Don Juan and the Power
of Medicine Dreaming

Don Juan and the Power of Medicine Dreaming

A NAGUAL WOMAN'S JOURNEY OF HEALING

MERILYN TUNNESHENDE

Bear & Company
Rochester, Vermont

Bear & Company
One Park Street
Rochester, Vermont 05767
www.InnerTraditions.com

Library of Congress Cataloging-in-Publication Data

Tunneshende, Merilyn.
    Don Juan and the power of medicine dreaming : a Nagual woman's journey of healing / Merilyn Tunneshende.
       p. cm.
    ISBN 1-879181-93-2 (pbk.)
    1. Tunneshende, Merilyn. 2. Juan, Don, 1891- 3. Shamans—Mexico—Biography. 4. AIDS (Disease)—Patients—Mexico—Biography. 5. Medicine, Magic, mystic, and spagiric—Mexico. 6. Nagualism. I. Title.
BF1598.T86 A3 2002
299'.93—dc21
                    2002000396

Printed and bound in Canada

10 9 8 7 6 5 4 3 2 1

Text design and layout by Rachel Goldenberg
This book was typeset in Legacy serif, with Legacy sans and Apolline as display typefaces

To don Juan,
doña Celestina,
Chon, and
Charley Spider

Contents

Introduction

~

The energetic focus of the work in this book is that of a shamanic dream journey, or a psychodrama of healing. This journey was actually undertaken by my mentors and me and it is filled to the brim with revelations about healing potential. We became pathfinders in the unknown, exploring new depths within the uncharted terrain of healing possibility.

The journey experience was comprised of awakened or lucid dreaming, followed by intended, cultivated, and spontaneous synchronicity in the waking world. These bridges were then crossed and the ongoing dreams were entered into with laserlike focus, in a state that we like to call "dreaming awake" that is akin to experiencing somnambulism with a heightened awareness. This state permits the body to fully partake of and actually walk into the dream, boots and all.

Although some people have natural capacities for this experience, they must be refined. But the instruction in how to do so has been a well-guarded secret. Thus, I have spent many years developing these facilities, utilizing practices that were learned under the guidance of extremely responsible and highly regarded shamans. I wish to express my gratitude to each and every one of these keenly powerful and wise women and men, and to all the sentient beings of every level who have helped, guided, or instructed me.

My intent in writing this book is to share the pure truth that there is much more to being than we are sometimes willing to allow or understand. These experiences, for all their magical, phenomenal nature, have been documented with complete sobriety and have, in fact, been followed up by hard science. Thus, you may feel confident to go on with the journey, in all its unforeseen permutations.

This newly revised edition has been refined to incorporate some very recent, groundbreaking energetic discoveries. We have now conclusively proved that the reality one experiences is very much affected by the energetic level in which one finds oneself, and that entire worldviews are based upon the description of reality as seen from that level. However, if one changes the level—the dream—and moves from, for example, a fear-based or a will-based worldview to a heart-based view, every meaning and every nuance changes radically. Essentially, the matrix supporting the old view dissolves.

My mentors and I undertook a journey to change the dream into true awakening. This book tells the story of our journey and allows the reader to gain a foothold in this transcendence. Individuals and groups from every walk of life, including psychologists, physicians, patients, artists, storytellers, feminists, theoretical physicists, and students of shamanism, have told me over the years that this work has changed their lives. It is a great joy to now offer the transfigured realizations herein.

Readers have also written to ask if it is possible for them to learn to experience the kind of states explored in this book. We have discovered that it is quite possible through conscientious experimentation and concerted teaching effort over a period of several years. We have also found that each person experiences and attains the states according to the purity of his or her own heart.

The heart and the path that helps purify it are key elements in this journey. This is not a mental exercise, although the mind is highly challenged by such experiences. Rather, the journey is about essences: incorruptibility, hope, courage, love, and altruism. It is the spiritual alchemy of turning intuition into wisdom and aggression into the sacrifice of ego and the development of selfless compassion.

I sincerely hope that each one of you, even if only for a moment, can glimpse the awesome wonder and the humbling beauty of standing naked and looking the unfathomable presence in the eye.

Part 1

Dreaming the Dream

C H A P T E R

one

❧

We had moved back to the South. The big lunar thrust in California had ended. It was here that I met and fell in love with Richard Morrison. Richard was a scholarship student from Northern Ireland, studying American writers at a small Southern college. I was then undecided as to my major, wavering between foreign languages and religion/philosophy.

Richard was my first physical intimacy, and I threw myself into it fully. I shocked my family by openly living with him in his apartment, completely moving out of my dormitory. I was mesmerized by him and he loved it, but he was also captivated with me. We were both voracious readers and fervently discussed the books we read. He was particularly intrigued by Jack Kerouac and William S. Burroughs, and I by Gabriel García Márquez and Carlos Castaneda.

After a reading by William S. Burroughs at our college,

we decided to take a trip to Mexico the summer after graduation. Mexico. By then, Richard would have a degree in English Literature and I in Spanish. The reading was principally of *Naked Lunch*, and it was followed by a party for the author at a private residence, which was also graced by Jerome, who had played piano for Billie Holiday.

We arrived at an exquisite lake home around nine. Mr. Burroughs was being deluged with questions while he stood in the galley kitchen. Richard and I quietly waited in the wings until, one by one, people became so embarrassed by their inability to begin meaningful conversation that they abandoned the author to us. Richard motioned for me to approach the author while Burroughs stared back at him hopefully.

I stepped forward and remarked, "The visual dimension of your writing is very stimulating."

Burroughs smiled and took a deep breath. "Is that fellow with you a writer?"

I nodded and waved Richard over while I made our introductions. We spoke as the three of us walked into the Florida room behind the grand piano. As we looked through the glass, the aquarium-like view of the sunken living room and of Jerome tickling the ivories under golden light was spellbinding.

Burroughs's voice whanged like a buzz saw. He told us a story about a gentleman in New York who sought him out after having an alien visitation. He was engrossed in telling Richard how the man had tried to convince Burroughs to utilize this experience in his writing. My attention was diverted by the music as I glanced away. When I finally looked back I interjected, "What was the message of the visitation?"

Burroughs turned to me with a smirk. He exhaled a long stream of smoke befitting the godfather of surrealism and let his unoccupied hand linger on the lapel of his conservative three-piece suit. "That's the part that's ludicrous. Up until then I was interested, even excited," he cracked. "Supposedly the shining dome hovers and illuminates 'H4' in the night sky." Burroughs's expression was totally deadpan. Richard coughed with laughter.

"H4? What kind of message is that?" I shook my head.

"Exactly," he gestured insanely with his arms. "That's where the whole thing crapped out. It was frustrating. I thanked him very much and excused myself."

"What a disappointment," I muttered. Just then a tipsy party diva, dressed in a flamboyant long gown concealing a barrel torso, traipsed over to him. "Oh, Mr. Burroughs, just take me around flying once." Burroughs groaned and chuckled, resisting the woman. He tried to stick to his spot, but he was slowly absorbed by another round of party guests.

Later in the evening Richard spent a long time talking with Burroughs in the Florida room. I sat in the sunken living room listening to the best jazz and blues piano I had ever heard. Afterward, on the way home, Richard could not stop talking. He had gotten Burroughs's secretarial address and was invited to send samples of his prose. They had also discussed at great length the use of travel as an inspiration for writing.

"I want us to go to Mexico after graduation, Merilyn," Richard said excitedly, as he drove our blue Volkswagen home through the dark streets. "With your skills in Spanish, we could get off the beaten path and really see a lot. I feel an intense experience would be good for my writing. You're always saying that Latin America is currently experiencing a Golden Age in its literature."

"You don't have to convince me, Richard. It's a great idea. Just promise me that what happened to Burroughs's lady down there won't happen to me," I said, as he glanced over at me. "The scene in his novel where he accidentally shoots her through the head is based on actual fact." I smiled coyly as I lit a Newport and blew the smoke out à la Garbo. Richard loved to watch me French-inhale, and I practically chain-smoked to entertain him.

It was May of our last semester and we began to occupy ourselves with preparations for the writers' trek to Mexico. We would take the train as far west as Yuma, Arizona, and then head south by bus, with every hamlet as our destination. We would become seasoned travelers, famous authors, and infamous lovers, all in one trip.

About two weeks before our planned departure I had to pick up Richard late at night after he had conducted an interview with a visiting rock band for the college paper. It was dark and windy as I made my way to our VW. I was very sleepy. While fumbling for the keys in my purse, I heard the most ungodly sound imaginable, a sound straight from the underworld, right out of a nightmare. Somehow it sensed that I had focused on it; it grew louder, modulating itself in horrible, prolonged twangs. I dropped the keys on the pavement and rushed back into our apartment, slamming and locking the door behind me. Then I hid in a dark corner, trembling.

The sound grew louder, ending in bloodcurdling screams and wails. I thought it must be a drunken ax murderess fresh from her foul deed. I had never before or since heard anything that compared to this sound. It created jagged, hollow gray images in my mind, like slivers of broken glass. I sweat acrid bullets and became nauseous. I must have shivered in the dark for an hour after the sound finally stopped.

I was terrified to leave our apartment. But I had to pick up Richard, who by now was no doubt concerned that something had happened to me. Summoning my courage I peeped out the door in the direction of the parking lot. At the spot where I had dropped my keys there was a strange small cat-like animal, but the front half was gray and the back half black. It appeared to deliberately move under a street lamp so I could see that its coloring was no optical illusion. Then, when I took a few steps forward, the animal disappeared.

A cold chill ran through me as I started the car. By the time I arrived at the club I was shaking so badly that I could not drive us back. I had the unmistakable feeling that this experience was some kind of warning, as if something were preparing to take its vengeance. While we sat in the running car I told Richard about the incident. As he listened all the color drained from his face. He muttered something about old stories from his homeland, about banshees, while he chain-smoked.

Then, as he stared out the window, Richard told me of a recurring dream that bothered him terribly. In the dream he is standing by a stalled car on the middle of deserted bridge at night. Suddenly a fast car with glaring lights bolts out of nowhere and barrels straight for him, mowing him down before he can jump out of the way. Richard told me that the headlights on this phantom car were stalking him like the eyes of death and that the banshees were messengers of death. He seemed supremely concerned, and his temples perspired heavily.

Later, after we returned home and went to bed, I slipped into a recurring dream that had haunted me since childhood. In the dream I am abandoned by my parents in the desert and I search for any sort of human contact. I cannot find anybody, only bones and cacti. The wind starts to whip up and pushes me around with its dry force. I can barely see through the flying sand. Finally, I spy a small shack in the distance and struggle to make my way to it. When I come upon the shack, I discover a tall, white-haired Native American man leaning against the gusts. "Grandfather! Grandfather!" I call to him. He motions desperately for me to go inside. The wind blows through the cracks in the boards, but we are safe.

Usually this is where the dream ended, but that night it continued. I asked Grandfather, "Where's Richard?" but he shook his head no. Then Richard sat up in bed, broken out in a cold sweat, and screamed us both awake.

Two nights later, while on our way home, we were in an automobile accident on a deserted road outside of town. We were returning from a concert Richard had covered, and our friend Eric Damon was driving his hatchback; I sat up front discussing the music with him. Richard was asleep on the back seat. The road was dark and ours was the only car on it. The white line was turning into a blur. I looked into the back; Richard was curled up in a fetal position. I smiled and let my head rest gently on my shoulder, still peeking at him over the seat. I drifted off to sleep.

I seemed to sense a spinning force hurling us off the road, and when I awoke we had already crashed. The windshield was shattered in slivers all around me, leaving the frame a gaping black hole. I was pinned down. I yelled, "I can't get out. Help!" My hand came up bloody. "Oh, God."

Eric came into view. He was walking alone in the middle of the forsaken road under a full moon. "Merilyn," he said, sticking his head through the driver's window. His face was cut.

"Eric, what happened? Where's Richard?" I screamed.

"He's lying on the road about a hundred yards back. He doesn't look good, Merilyn. The hatch must've flown open when we went off the road. Don't know how long ago this happened. But I flagged down a car and they went to call an ambulance."

I began to scream inconsolably.

The ambulance arrived a few minutes later, and rescuers worked with a blowtorch to remove my door off the side of the crushed car. It took about twenty minutes to extricate me, and I was then taken straight to the waiting vehicle. Eric was right. Richard did not look well. He was already inside under an oxygen mask. He was very pale. His eyes and head were rolling and he had a queer expression on his face, as if someone had told him the most sickly sweet yet sarcastic joke in the world. We made desperate eye contact all the way to the emergency room, but he died on the operating table of internal bleeding shortly after our arrival.

They medicated Eric and me and told us nothing. We

were sent home after doctors stitched our heads and tended to our other injuries. Eric's mother was waiting at my apartment to tell us the news. When I saw her I realized what had happened and tried to run for my car and race back to the hospital, but I fell to the ground in convulsions.

Richard came from a poor Irish background and was survived by only an uneducated widowed mother. It was impossible to contact her in time so I had to make all the funeral arrangements. When she was finally notified she was afraid that the trip would be more than she could bear, even though I offered to pay for her passage.

I was a hollow ghost haunting the apartment and weeping for hours over one of Richard's shoes or a favorite book. I could not find his poetry anywhere. At night I would lie in a heap of his clothes and roll through them hysterically, searching with my fingers as if looking for my lost eyes. Finally, my mother came to my aid.

One night she walked into the bedroom looking somber. "You've got to get out of here, Merilyn. He left you his savings, didn't he? Be free. That's what he'd have wanted. A conventional life was never for you. Especially not now. You listen to me." She took off her scarab bracelet, her only mystery, and gave it to me.

"Yes, mother," I choked, wiping my hot face in anguish.

A little less than two weeks later, in total shock, we went

to the Maple Hill Cemetery on a windswept and rainy afternoon and observed the placement of a pyramid cast in bronze
that I had commissioned as his headstone. It had no date of
death and no year of birth, only the date of birth, November 5,
and the inscription in French: Pour Richard (for Richard).

two

~

All the arrangements for the trip to Mexico had been made prior to Richard's death. In its wake, my shattered self embraced the venture fully. It was our dream and I intended to live it. Richard had left me his small life savings—ten thousand dollars. All he had in this world. It would be spent in his honor. I would see for him and write what he could no longer pen. Hopefully, it would in some small way fulfill his hopes and dreams.

It was a long, sad train trip. Grim. I cried most of the way, staring at a hazy landscape through smudged, tearstained windows. But when the train crossed into Arizona and I saw that desert again, as if for the first time, I had an inexplicable feeling of renewed anticipation. It felt as if my whole reality was being pulled by something or someone, traveling through an endless dark tunnel to a predetermined destination.

It was sunset and we were traveling close to the border, near Nogales. The colors were spectacular. As we journeyed deeper into Arizona I would occasionally spy Papago women around small, solitary houses off in the distance. Their fires were smoking against the rose-golden semicircular sun sinking below the horizon. Saguaros stretched their arms and yawned at the evening. Shadows melted. Crows flew to their last low perches of the day and blinked at the coming twilight.

It was totally dark when the train pulled into Yuma. The air was dry and there was a warm breeze. I pulled down my overstuffed backpack from above my seat as the engine made those end-of-destination noises. At first I did not see him when I stepped out of the car onto the darkened platform. He was wearing black slacks and a black tunic and had his hair tied back with a black bandanna around the forehead. Something inside me would not let me take my eyes off him. I even set down my rucksack and just stood and stared. He was tall, quiet, still. Standing in the shadows with his eyes glinting like a feline was the old Indian I had often dreamed of as a child. It was Grandfather!

For me that old Indian, John Black Crow, or don Juan in Spanish, was the beginning and end of all things. As I walked away from the station with him, I remember thinking that my life would never be the same. I was right.

"You come stay with me," the old Indian said as he

approached me. He seemed to have been waiting for some-one, and I wondered if he had mistaken me for her. "The only hotel near the train station is that one." He pointed to the shambles of a distant, rambling two-story building from the thirties. By the light of a street lamp, I could just make out the screens peeling off the second-floor hospitality porch. I shuddered. "It's a rat trap," he continued. "And it's late. You won't find a cab tonight. Besides, the reservation is much more interesting." He pointed into the dark in the other direction. "I'm an old man. I won't bite."

I marveled at the speed and skill with which this Native American was trying to pick me up. He was forceful about it. Imperious. It was like the desperate gesturing in my dream. I felt this old spirit pulling me from an underworld into which I had fallen, and I sensed that he was my only hope to avoid complete annihilation.

In a state of culture shock, I agreed with a nod of my head. My other prospects were less appealing in this small desert town that night. He flashed me a mischievous smile and then turned around to lead the way. The desert wind began to pick up and a waning moon came out from be-hind a solitary cloud. The sparse plant life and night birds seemed to come to life mysteriously, making whispering sounds or soft lingering cries. I headed off trustfully into the night with a man I had met only in my dreams.

"You follow me," he said, as we crossed a bridge and trudged up a dirt road, leaving the practically deserted train-station platform. Don Juan, a Yuma Indian, lived in a clap-board house on the reservation. He appeared to be about eighty-five years old. I adjusted the pack on my back and looked behind me in the moonlight. We were hiking up a road that curved around a barren hill. At the top of the hill, to the right of the road, was a large, bleached-out dead tree in the shape of a bent fork. Down the road on the left, I saw a solitary store lit by one dim bulb. We descended into the bubble of its light as we came closer and closer, floating on silent feet.

We stopped at the small establishment. Don Juan asked if I needed to buy anything, and then stood by the cash box at the front and talked with a Native American man who was blind in one eye. I scoured the place for anything edible. All I found were fried pork rinds, beef jerky, and a few packs of crackers hidden between cans of kerosene, metal wire, tires, and cigarettes. I settled for the crackers and a bottle of Coke. When I walked to the front to pay, I asked don Juan if he wanted anything. He shook his head.

Long Silence Emerson, the man introduced to me at the cash box, brushed back his short salt-and-pepper hair with his fingers as he sat on a stool. He smiled and stared back at me with one good and one silvery eye. I handed him the money and put the food in my rucksack. Don Juan was lean-ing against the counter. He seemed to be showing me off, or maybe he was just snickering at the pitiful supplies I had selected.

After we said goodnight we walked another mile around a bend and down the road until I saw a tiny, squalid settlement of trailers and clapboard houses illuminated by a few streetlights. "Here we are," don Juan said as he ambled down a slope toward a small house set off by itself.

Don Juan's house sat between a sandy hill, which partially shielded it from the road, and an irrigation ditch in the back. After he opened the door and we went inside, I discovered that he did not have electricity. The one-room dwelling was lit by kerosene lanterns. In the dim light I noticed two wooden bunks at opposite ends of the room. Each bunk had a large wooden slat window at the foot. These were the only windows in the small house. One opened to the front facing the hill, the other to the back overlooking the water. Don Juan pointed to the bunk facing the water and told me that was mine.

I placed my belongings on the bed. The mattress sounded like it was made of straw. The bed was covered by a cotton blanket with thunderbolt designs across it in indigo and yellow. More blankets were doubled at the foot. Don Juan lit another lantern. I saw that the designs on his blankets were like stars exploding in the center.

In the middle of the room stood an unfinished wood table and two benches. Against the back wall was a wooden stool, a double gas burner, and two crude wooden chests. At the back was another door exactly opposite the one at the front. And in the dim light I detected woven bags, which appeared to be filled with dried plants, hanging from the rafters.

Don Juan told me that I should get some rest, because in the morning we might take a walk in the desert. He indicated that the plumbing was outside in the back. I pulled some plaid flannel pajamas out of my bag along with a toothbrush and paste and went out back.

Not far from the irrigation ditch, its water reflecting the moon, there was a spigot for washing. To the side was an outside shower stall and, off by itself, a water closet. There were a few wooden folding chairs leaning against the house. I brazenly entered the water closet and changed into my pajamas.

When I returned, don Juan was sitting at the table and chuckling softly to himself. His laughter made me uncomfortable, but nevertheless I felt safe and slipped into my bunk. I was exhausted. The train trip had taken about thirty-six hours, and I had not slept the whole time.

The mattress was definitely straw. Don Juan had opened the windows and a delicate night breeze blew over me. As he turned out the lanterns I heard an owl hoot in the distance. While I drifted off to sleep I listened to don Juan chanting in the dark. That night I dreamed for the first time of the Mayan culture.

I am with don Juan walking in a forest. We spy through the foliage what appears to be the ancient ruins of Palenque, as I recall them from picture books. We proceed along the path. I seem to be myself but I wear a long black braid and a white tunic.

We come to a clearing where there stands a bronze, lean, and muscular middle-aged man who also wears a white tunic. His dark hair is cropped with bangs and he is smiling. Obviously, he is awaiting us. The man tells me that I am dreaming and that dreams are how they keep track of me. He introduces himself in Maya (which I seem to understand) as the Chuch Kaháu, the timekeeper, and tells me that don Juan is Uay Kin, the shapeshifter sun. He says that the three of us have a destiny to fulfill.

We walk together. The dense plant life is flowering and very fragrant. Amid the vines on the ground we come upon a massive, abandoned stone disk calendar. The Chuch Kaháu bends over and pulls the vines away from it. He then takes tamarind seeds from a pod on a nearby tree and casts them onto the giant disk. The seeds roll into carved hieroglyphic niches and grooves, like marbles on a roulette wheel. The Chuch Kaháu tells me to read the dates indicated. Somehow I can interpret the Mayan glyphs. One date is my birth date and the other is the last date on the calendar.

"Why does the calendar stop here?" I ask, looking back at the Chuch Kaháu. He motions for me to look at the calendar again. Its grooves are beginning to bleed. Soon there is a stream of blood at our feet. The seeds then turn into butterflies, which flutter away.

A popping sound follows, and I hear the Chuch Kaháu say, "When this happens, you will know. Seek out Kukulkán." Then he waves goodbye and recedes into the green foliage. Don Juan walks a bit farther into the forest and finds an enormous spider web with a hole in its center. He indicates for me to follow him through the opening.

When I reached the other side I woke up in bed. First light was seeping into the last moment of desert night as seen from my window. Don Juan was sitting cross-legged on a small thunderbird rug by his bunk, hauntingly playing a river cane flute.

"That's beautiful, don Juan," I said, stretching my arms. A cool morning breeze blew through the window. He put down the flute and smiled at me. Its music seemed to have awakened me from my sadness as well as my sleep. "I had the most unsettling dream." I turned on my left side to look straight at him. "I dreamed that I was with you and another Native American walking through the forest." He merely nodded his head, encouraging me to tell him the rest of the dream.

"In the dream I was a Native American myself and understood the Mayan language of southern Mexico. I saw an ancient calendar and was able to interpret it." I propped myself on my elbow.

Sunlight touched don Juan's iridescent silvery-white hair, which now hung loose in thick feathers that reached his jaw. He was still wearing his black shirt and slacks and had a peculiar, thoughtful expression on his aquiline face. He stretched one leg out and bent the other at the knee, draw-ing it to his chest. Don Juan took his time commenting on my dream as he leaned against his bunk.

"I know something about this," he finally said.

"Excuse me?"

"That dream. What if I told you that you're not the only person who has dreams like that? I have them myself, and they mean something."

"I guess, since you were there," I added.

He smiled tolerantly and waved me off. "What if I told you I know the other person in that dream? That is how I found you. Why do you think you came with me so easily?"

I was dumbfounded. I stared at the old Indian with a blank expression on my face. I had heard about this type of thinking among the Native Americans but had not expected to encounter it so soon. Or perhaps I did.

"I suppose . . ." I began cautiously, measuring my words, "that considering the things that have happened to me re-cently, I've got nothing to lose by listening to you, or even acknowledging what you say—partially. But I don't know. I've had some bad shocks."

He chuckled and stood up. "In the old days people used to cultivate special dreams."

"What do these dreams mean?" I was now more than a little curious.

"How about some breakfast?" he asked, completely changing the subject.

"I'm starved." I was somewhat relieved to stop this discussion.

Don Juan removed an earthenware pot from one of the wooden chests, filled it with water, and placed it on a burner to make herbal tea. Next he took down a dried plant from one of the hanging woven bags. On the other burner he set another clay pot with water for cornmeal mush. From the same chest he pulled out two carved wooden bowls decorated with stylized roadrunners, two black pottery mugs, several spoons, cornmeal, some dates, and a small buckskin bundle.

He patted the bench in front of the table for me to sit down. "Eat the dates with the meat. Then the mush." He opened a piece of plastic wrap containing the dates, then the buckskin cloth holding pieces of dried deer meat, lightly coated in a red chili powder. "Do you like deer jerky?" he asked as he placed the open packages on the table.

"I love it," I assured him, even though I had never tried it.

"I hunt the deer myself." He stepped over to turn down the tea water.

"What's in the other chest?" I asked.

He ignored me, pouring out a bitter brown liquid. "Isn't this enough food?" he finally responded, raising his eyebrows.

"Oh, gosh. Yes," I said in chagrin.

"Those are my toys," he continued, casting his eyes toward the second chest. I assumed he meant personal items and sacred objects. He sounded like a little child and pursed his lips as he said "toys."

I inquisitively glanced over at the closed chest while he served me a bowl of mush. He caught my look and grinned. "Eat," he said, lightly slapping my fingers on the table as he pulled up a bench and sat down opposite me.

We munched our breakfast in silence. When we finished he stood up. "Help me clean up. Then change. We'll take a walk before it gets too hot. There's a lot to see in the desert morning. We can continue our conversation about dreams."

After breakfast we walked along the irrigation ditch for an hour and then headed into the brush. Don Juan showed me swirling backward-S tracks in the sand. "These are rattle-snake tracks," he said, pointing with a stick. "They come to the ditch at night to drink the water. During the day they stay under the rocks. There're many different kinds of animal life around here. What animal would you say you're like?" He sat down on a nearby boulder.

I leaned against it, facing the small trading post in the distance. I thought I understood what he meant. "I guess I'm a cat. I used to dream, when I was kid, of racing through the blackness of night, pushing through low leaves to the river. I always had black spots on dark forearms and paws." I showed him the birthmark on my left inside forearm. "When I'd come to the river a funny little man would be there drinking water. I'd get angry at that and pounce on his chest, knocking him onto his back. Then, instead of going for his throat, I'd lick his face and stare at him. He'd scream, scared silly. I'd jump off him and saunter over to drink from the cool water, and he'd run off into the jungle yelling at the top of his lungs."

Don Juan laughed out loud. "Sounds like a black jaguar to me. They're from that area of Mexico you dreamed about last night. Big cats always watch the watering holes at night for prey but most won't kill a man, just attack and maim him. But you just licked him, huh?"

"How do you know so much about animals, don Juan?" I was fascinated.

"In my tradition we're taught to dream so thoroughly about our power animals that we can become or shift into those animals in our Dreaming, and there receive wisdom and visions. Here one is referred to as a shapeshifter. Across the border in Mexico, one with this ability is called a *nagual.* Our helpers can also come and tell us what is happening, the good and bad things that affect us. If I were you I wouldn't tell anybody about your power animal yet. Jaguar is powerful medicine. You have the facility; perhaps I'll tell you more about this kind of Dreaming if you stay in the area awhile." Don Juan pulled a bandanna out of his pocket to shield his tan brow. I began to feel tired and a little sad, recalling my quandary.

We moved over to another boulder and sat in its shade.

Don Juan became as strangely quiet as the stone itself. At first I attributed his silence to the impinging morning heat, then I noticed my own stillness. Suddenly I realized that he had tapped into the depth of my anguish and it had silenced him. I felt my tears welling up but I could not cry. Instead I began to float, suspended in their watery depth. I looked at don Juan and saw a peaceful, brilliant energy radiating around him. Comfort. I sank into it. He understood everything.

I became so quiet that I could perceive bubbles between moments of existence, as if the whole of life were dissolving into them. I began to weep deeply. Don Juan's voice rippled with sadness. "Don't cry. Go into the silence," he said.

The following morning, after walking in the desert for several hours and returning to don Juan's house, we got ready for a trip into town. He and I alternately took long cool showers and washed our hair with mashed yucca root that he had quickly prepared. I slipped into khaki shorts and a matching shirt, braided by wet hair, and put on a straw hat to shield my face from the sun. Don Juan came back inside, also dressed in khaki. He wore trousers and a short-sleeved shirt. "We match," he joked, and then inserted a puma claw earring into his ear.

Don Juan led me across the reservation bridge. The town of Yuma was spread out and fairly modern. He told me that they had cowboy bars, health food stores, and Mexican restaurants. In the winter months many elderly people flocked to the city and its trailer courts in search of the mild temperatures.

We stepped into a darkly lit, 1930s-period poolroom saloon with ceiling fans and huge pictures of Clark Gable and Greta Garbo on the walls. We ordered two iced teas at the fountain/bar, then sat down at a wooden table and watched the pool players. Don Juan told me that during the hottest months of the year he was a fixture in this place.

"So what part of Mexico are you going to?" he asked, sipping his tea.

"Guess I'll go all the way down and start in the Yucatán with the ruins I dreamed about. Then I can work my way back up. That seems to make sense," I said, sticking my nose into the icy glass.

"Sounds like a good plan," don Juan said. Some off-duty Air Force types were staring across the room at the girl with the old Indian. "Don't worry about them," don Juan said in a low voice. "I'm like the wooden Indian in the tobacco shop to them. When they see me they just make jokes. If they ask I'll tell them you're my niece." They did not ask any questions.

We spent the hottest part of the day there, listening to tunes on the jukebox and talking. After it cooled off, we took the bus to San Luis Rio Colorado on the Mexican border and ate our fill of *machaca* burritos at an outdoor food stand. "San Luis is where you'll start your trip," don Juan said. "When you're ready, I'll take you to the border myself."

As we rode back to Yuma on the bus, we passed the date plantations of the Cocopah Reservation. Don Juan opened the window and let the dusty but fresh air blow into our faces, while we gazed at the colors of sunset in the sky over the now-fertile, irrigated sections of desert.

During my stay with him I did not ask don Juan many questions about his past. He offered very little in reply. According to him, he was born before the turn of the century and was taught a lot by his grandmother, who still remembered life before the westward expansion. His mother died when he was eleven and he was left an orphan. He was then sent to the military-mission elementary school. During the Mexican revolution of 1910 he crossed back into Mexico to fight for Indian lands. While there don Juan stole an Indian woman for his bride. Unbeknownst to him, she had recently given birth, and the baby died in her absence. He solemnly returned the woman to her people. Because of this tragedy he never married or had children. Years later, don Juan returned to Arizona.

About my past, don Juan wanted to know only where I was born and what the land was like. He did listen carefully to my story about Richard Morrison and was convinced that Richard and I had an agreement of power that would "put me on the path to him," as he put it. I felt that don Juan valued our contact more than words could express, but he spoke few of them. I have never met a more fiercely alone being—or a stronger one.

We did, however, talk repeatedly about the strange dream I had the first night in his home. Don Juan was reluctant to tell me it's meaning, although I sensed he knew it. But during our talks he disclosed certain ancient Dreaming practices, which piqued my curiosity about his broader knowledge of such things. For now I was content merely to be his friend. At don Juan's suggestion I stayed with him indefinitely in one of the earth's hottest spots. After all, like him I was completely alone.

Don Juan was essentially a silent being. He did not toss and turn when he slept. He did not move randomly when awake or waste words when he spoke. We spent many days without speaking a word, just sinking more deeply into one another. I would accompany him on walks in the desert or into town or by the irrigation canals. He did not work in the summer, but I sensed that he did odd jobs throughout the region during the other three seasons.

If there were chores to perform we did them together and he would patiently show me the procedure. I learned to clean a fish, find mussels, dry plants and fruits, rake sand, and play a flute, among other incidental things. Somehow, he acquired a small blackboard and chalk so I could help the Yuman children with their English. Occasionally, he would lie under a tree singing softly, and several children would gather at the edge of the ring formed by the sound of his voice. When he finished don Juan would stand up, dust himself off, and walk away. They would then scurry over and ask me to write a word on the little blackboard.

Don Juan and I often sat still next to one another for hours, leaning against a boulder and gazing at a distant sandstone formation that looked like two cloaked beings, the smaller leaning against the larger. We would gaze into the river until we melted away, or we would watch herons glide and then land and wade for shell creatures. Often we lay on our backs under trees and stared at the clouds while he chanted, or we would follow the flight of a flock of crows with our awareness. Slowly we became the sandstone, the river, the herons, the clouds, the crows.

The native people on the reservation began whispering among themselves about Dream Power. They sensed what don Juan was doing with me. When I was "completely silent" and the world was "still," don Juan showed me circular hand and arm motions that were for "pulling and circulating" energy. The movements reminded me of conjuring over a boiling cauldron.

Next I was instructed to Dream, both while asleep and awake, of a circulating spiral in front of me, pulling and shifting the air and water, the clouds, the energy, and the earth itself through it. We practiced on the formation of sandstone pillars on the horizon. Don Juan said I should pull them through the spiral and attempt to manifest them somewhere else. I don't know if it was the absolute silence, the power of his presence, or even my dreams, but his words made perfect sense to me.

He told me how he could pull energy through a dark tunnel to him. What he was explaining, he said, was very visionary and could be perceived only with the eye between the eyebrows. I then remembered the dark-tunnel sensation I experienced on the train to Yuma. It had reminded me of the reported near-death experience of light at the end of the tunnel. Any questions about his methods were forever banished, as this confirmed his power. In time I began to perceive a glowing silver cord of energy coming out of my umbilicus. Whatever I was "pulling" would explode into physical manifestation somewhere and then grow, circulate, and evolve.

I sometimes pondered what kind of being walked this path. One night my curiosity overwhelmed me. We were lying on our bunks with the slat windows open. The moon was shining through his window, showering him with light. I slipped out of my bed and furtively tiptoed over to don Juan. He was lying on his back, still as a stone and as silent. I lay down beside him and could sense the muscular hardness of his body. Suddenly I saw a silvery golden light under his closed eyelids; the spheres began to roll in my direction. I nuzzled even closer.

The sensation felt like being beside a Roman candle. Golden energy rushed up from him, expanded, and enveloped me like a blanket. I melted and became a golden rippling pond, pulsating with the awareness of my own being. We stayed entwined in this energy until the sun rose and we both opened our eyes, me first followed by him a second later.

That was don Juan. Our dance was at once elegant, intimate, exquisite, and mostly silent. We absorbed each other. We burned through each other. Never in my life have I felt such a profound and powerful melding with another being. To define our bond in terms of personal love would be like comparing the radiance of a light bulb to that of the sun.

We knew there was something infinite between us. It was forever. He spoke my language better than anyone, and I was truly the only one who could fully understand his. And as he promised, one day don Juan took me to the border at San Luis Rio Colorado. "Go. Do. Be. Seek. Come back when the spirit moves you," he said. "You'll find me here."

It was a beautiful, clear afternoon. I desired to stay with him even longer. I was captivated by him and absorbed by how much I loved and trusted him. Then an unfamiliar curiosity stirred in me, like breath from ashes, and I glanced across the Colorado River Bridge into Mexico. He stood at the edge of the bridge as I walked across.

CHAPTER
three

〜

Walking into old Mexico as a young, recently "widowed" woman, I felt like a sacrificial offering. Rough men in straw hats ready to stake their claim on females stood on dusty street corners outside crude, squat buildings. Some leered at me and called out. I asked directions and made my way to the nearby train station. The daily train was almost ready for departure.

No experience can prepare you for a ride on a second-class Mexican train—unless you have ridden on a second-class Mexican train. I sat down in my seat only to discover that the window was broken out—and it does grow cold in the desert at night. The good seats with intact windows had already been taken by modest Mexican country women and their children or by rugged men in straw hats and boots.

Actually, the word "seat" was a misnomer. They were merely hard wooden benches with backs.

I was told that this second-class train would take twice as long to reach Mexico City as a first-class train because it stopped in every little village along the way. It was useless asking for a refund; the whole thirty-hour trip cost only ten dollars. As I looked around in despair, I noticed that most people were well stocked for the trip. Almost everyone had a plastic net tote stuffed with toilet paper, thin blankets, food, and wet bandannas for wiping their hands and faces.

Mexico's more primitive nature seemed attuned to my inner state, yet the overall culture shock was totally numbing. The train pulled out and chugged across the Mexican desert for about an hour and then stopped every thirty minutes for the rest of the trip. At least the breeze was pleasant.

Each time the train arrived at a station vendors of all ages, their plastic washtubs stuffed with homemade goods, would descend on us and cram the aisles hawking their wares. *"Tamales calientes!"* *"Churros!"* *"Cerveza fria!"* Some of the food actually looked quite good, and the people sitting around me smiled in approval when I broke down and bought a chicken tamale. An elderly woman handed me a damp paper napkin from her bag.

Using a lavatory, if it was a lavatory, was an experience. These toilets were basically foul-smelling water closets without water. Given the high level of usage and the jouncing of the train, they looked more like animal stalls. The floor in the one I used was wet and sticky. I held my breath and finished quickly, exploding out the door and taking a huge breath in one motion. Some of the Mexicans watched me and laughed good-naturedly.

As evening approached, the vendors' wares changed. Now they were selling thin blankets and strong coffee with sugar. The mountains were visible to the east, but we were still traveling through the desert. I decided it would be smart to buy a blanket for ten dollars, but I found it impossible to sleep and availed myself of the coffee stops.

During the night the makeup of the passengers changed from that of a northern desert person to one of a more southerly appearance. Boots were replaced by homemade sandals called *huaraches*. The tamales went from being wrapped in corn husks and stuffed with chicken to ones wrapped in slick, juicy banana leaves and stuffed with vegetables. I gorged myself on these new tamales.

As the sun rose, we were entering a lush tropical mountain area. The foliage extended to the windows of the train. Mist hung in the early morning air. This was Tepic in the state of Nayarit, halfway to Mexico City. The people here were simpler and even friendlier than those in the north. The robust women wore colorful shawls called *rebozos* wrapped around their shoulders over peasant blouses. Their arms were bronzed and strong. In the north the colors of the rebozos were drab, and in general the dress was more citified, though simple.

A woman seated in front of me leaned over to tell me that the train would turn and head east when we reached Guadalajara, then continue in that direction until we reached the capital of Mexico. I wondered if it would be easy to make a connection to the town of Palenque, how long that trip would be, and if there was a first-class train with cushioned seats and window glass.

Late that evening the train pulled into the modern station of the Districto Federal, as the Mexicans call their capital. It took more than an hour and a half to travel at modest speed over the city tracks to the railway platforms. I got the impression that Mexico City was almost infinite, sophisticated yet totally barbaric—an Aztec anthill of such colossal proportions that it could no longer be conceived except by Coatlicue, the creator-destroyer goddess who gave birth to it.

The ancient Aztec capital on which Mexico City was later built by its conquerors was originally called Tenochtitlán, and it was founded at the site of a prophesied apparition. The Aztecs were told that their capital would be established where they saw an eagle devouring a serpent on a cactus in the middle of a lake. The Aztec people were tenacious, vast, and warlike, and they had an obsession with death. Mexico City bears their lingering warrior presence.

The Capital Station's grand salon was bustling with activity. There were large directories of trains heading every-where. On the southbound board, I discovered a train listed for Palenque that would leave at midnight. It was about 9:00 P.M. and I decided to wait out the time in the station and depart for Palenque that night. I went to the southbound window and asked the clerk for a one-way first-class ticket. He told me the whole train was first class and that they even had a few Pullman cars. Since I had not slept in two days, I jumped at the chance for a train berth with a bed and a private bathroom.

Being able to move around made the wait bearable. I went into a restaurant and ordered chicken enchiladas and a cup of *atole*, a hot cornmeal drink flavored with vanilla and cinnamon or chocolate. Afterward I found the designated track and stood in line to board the train. The people in line looked like yet another type of Mexican. Most of the men were dressed in white slacks and tunic shirts with sandals. Some carried machetes and woven bags. Many of the women wore brightly embroidered white tunic dresses and gaily woven multicolored rebozos.

I noticed one man who was extremely striking. He was medium-sized, bronzed and trim yet muscular. He wore a tunic, slacks, and sandals, but his tunic was turquoise, not white. His straw hat reminded me of those worn in the rice paddies of Vietnam, with a little horsehair tassel swinging on the back of it. He was carrying a woven bag of dried plants and he bent over to arrange something inside it. He apparently saw me watching him out of the corner of his eye.

All at once he turned around flamboyantly to face me, removing his hat with a sweep and flourish and bringing it to his side. His blue-black hair hung a little shorter than his jaw, and his cropped bangs came down nearly to his eyebrows. His grin was large, white, and wide, almost from ear to ear. His ears were pierced and the holes fitted with small jade plugs. He also had a string of jade beads around his throat.

I rubbed my eyes in disbelief. This man closely resembled the Mayan in my jungle dream with don Juan! I dropped my bags, stopped dead, and just stared at him with my mouth gaping. Perspiration began to form on my palms and my stomach churned. I figured that I must have been completely exhausted and imagining the similarity. Suddenly, I felt water in my bowels and rushed off to the ladies' facilities. He just stood there grinning and watching me flee, as I disappeared around the corner of the platform.

When I slunk back and peeped around the corner the man stood in place adjusting his sack again. He looked up at me while tying a knot in a hemp rope that bound his large bundle. He smiled from under the brim of his hat and then straightened up and took a few steps toward me. I braced myself and stood still, practically paralyzed. He stopped and cocked his head, listening to the announcement of our train's departure.

Several young men dressed in white tunics and slacks rushed toward him, speaking in a language that was not Spanish and had a lot of clicks. They seemed to treat him with deference. The group of them had short dark hair and very finely chiseled beaklike noses. I swore I heard them say "Chuch," the Mayan name from my dream. They picked up his sack and carried it onto a train car.

The train was called again and I hurried onto the Pullman car that was behind the one the man and his companions had boarded. As the train pulled out I slipped into my pajamas and climbed into the sleeping berth. I was too weary to reflect on the events of the day, and after we left Mexico City and headed into the hills the darkness of the compartment and the rhythmic movement of the train lulled me to sleep.

In the morning my compartment was warm and stuffy. I stuck my head out into the hallway, and a passing conductor told me we were about ten hours from Palenque. The area was densely vegetated and broken up by cities and towns. Having slept for nearly half the trip I was starving, so I quickly washed, dressed, and moseyed into the next car to await the vendors.

The first-class cars had vinyl upholstered seats and window glass. There was also a visible improvement in cleanliness. I was told this train did not stop as often as the second-class, and so I had a short wait until we arrived at the next big town. I walked up the aisle looking for a seat. On my right, about halfway up the car, I passed the man from the train station and his companions occupying two seats. They were chomping on pistachios. The man smiled at me as I walked past. It appeared that the only available seat was in front of his. When I turned around, he engagingly patted the top of that seat with one hand while spitting out a shell into the other.

"Are you hungry, girly?" he asked in oddly accented Spanish as I sat down.

"I'm hoping for tamales!" I replied, speaking for my stomach.

He and his three companions burst out laughing. "Maybe they'll have yucca tamales with almonds. Have you tried those? They're my favorites."

From the seat behind him one of his companions called out, "I like the pineapple tamales with raisins." They all smiled. "These are my nephews—Eligio, Tiófilo, and Ignacio," said the older man. "My nickname is Chon. They're from the area around Palenque, but I'm originally from an area near Tayasal or, as it is now called, Flores, Guatemala, which is close to the ruins of Tikal. Do you know the ruins?"

"That's one of the reasons I came to Mexico."

"Really?" Chon asked in feigned surprise, his eyebrows raised.

"Yes," I continued. "I want to see what has been. I'm not so keen on what is." My tone was rather dejected.

"That's the best reason to come," Chon said, his tone strangely soothing. "Yes, things have changed but the temples are still precious marvels!" Chon spoke with strong emotion. I instinctively liked this man.

The train was stopping in the damp hill town of San Andres Tuxtla in the state of Veracruz. The awaited tamale vendors boarded the train. "They have yucca tamales!" Eligio exclaimed. He bought enough for all of us, and I thanked him profusely.

"It's a good thing we knew what to pick," Chon commented. "This area is full of wizards, and who knows what they put in their food."

I allowed that comment to pass, munching on my tamale as the train chugged through the hilly area of pueblos called the Tuxtlas. The group was quiet for a few minutes while we ate and then relaxed, gazing out the windows at the thick, green vegetation.

"This area is very damp," Chon began, tapping my back and shoulder. "A lot of moisture means many mosquitoes for you."

"Mosquitoes don't like me that much." I turned in my seat to face him again.

"Oh, these will!" he snickered. "Do you have a hammock and a mosquito net?"

"No, I was planning on staying at a hotel."

"You won't like them," Eligio said from his seat. "No fresh air."

Chon opened his eyes wide and stared at me. "What? You'll be too far to walk to the ruins. The town of Palenque is about seven miles away, and you'll only be able to see the sites during government hours. The best time to visit is in the early morning or at twilight when there are no people. That's what the Maya in the area do."

"But I don't know anyone nearby who'd put me up." I saw where this might lead, and as a solo female I was being cautious.

"There're camping grounds, but they're still a little far. My sister, Esmeralda, the mother of these three," Chon said nodding at his nephews, "has a place about a mile north of the ruins. She runs a small roadside restaurant. That's where we're going. I'll stay for a while, but these fellows will go to their own homes. You're welcome to stay with us."

"Oh, I couldn't possibly, I mean . . ." I stammered, looking away.

"Of course you can! You don't know much about us. That's why you feel uncomfortable. I understand, but strangers stay often," Chon argued.

"Uncle Chon is a healer," Ignacio proclaimed. "People from all over the Mayan area come for his cures and many stay for days. My mother even had archaeologists from the university stay with her. She's used to it, believe me. When he visits, Uncle Chon has a hut he uses just for his patients, and if it's vacant you can stay there and have privacy."

Chon seemed a little shy about his nephew's disclosure. He turned to me when Ignacio was finished. "We have hammocks and nets. You can pay my sister for meals. She's a very good cook. There's a waterfall about a mile from the hut that's great for bathing. And we can explore the ruins in the evening after my patients leave. I'm a very good guide and I won't charge you much."

His offer appeared genuine, and it was apparent to me that he was kind and trustworthy. His nephews were also very well-mannered. A good family. I had heard that in Mexico *"mi casa es su casa"* (my house is your house) was a philosophy and it was considered rude to refuse a sincere invitation. I felt a little uneasy about it but cautiously accepted the offer. His nephews whooped. They told me that their uncle would most likely be very busy during the day and that I should explore the ruins with them as well.

"When the people of the region hear that uncle Chon is there they'll start lining up," Tiófilo said, sitting down beside me.

"I went to see a friend who lives outside of Toluca in the state of Mexico," Chon added as an explanation. "That's how I came to be in the train station. My friend is an herbalist. He collects medicinal plants specific to that area. He always gifts me with many of them when I visit him. They're in the sack I'm carrying with me." Chon wore a sly little grin.

There were about eight more hours before we arrived at

Palenque. Chon's nephews retrieved their hats from the baggage racks above the seats and placed them over their faces to take naps. I excused myself and went back to my compartment to do the same. It was 7:00 P.M. when the conductor announced our arrival. I was eating another round of tamales. I quickly finished up, grabbed my backpack, and walked to the next car to exit the train with Chon and his nephews.

It was very humid on the platform. The twilight filtering through the dense jungle had a greenish hue. An attractive, robust middle-aged woman with gray-streaked black braids down to her strong hips, waved to us and sauntered over. Her smile was very engaging. She was neither extremely dark nor pale but a luminous mixture. The woman wore a cotton tunic dress with open lace panels above the chest and at the short sleeves, and she had on plastic sandals.

"What's up, Chon?" she said in Spanish, stepping up and kissing him on the cheek. She now smiled at me, "Is she with you?"

"Yes, Esmeralda. Merilyn, this is my sister." The two of them did not look like brother and sister. In fact, they looked so different that it must have been a family joke.

"Is she going to stay in the hut?" Esmeralda asked coyly.

"Yes." Chon replied.

"Well, you're welcome," Esmeralda said to me, nodding her head. "Chon, there's a woman with a baby who's been waiting for you. I think he may have *susto* [fright]," she added. Looking back at me she now pecked her boys on the cheek in a perfunctory manner and then strode off with us following after her. At the bus stop we made polite conversation, standing with our bags beneath the darkening sky.

"When we arrive home I'll fix you something wonderful to eat," Esmeralda said effusively, as if food were a magical act of love. Her heart seemed to swell in her chest and she clasped her hands there. She was very beautiful and gracious. I felt that I had made a good choice.

On the way out of town we passed a large public sculpture. It was a bust of the most famous ruler of Palenque, Pacal Votán, who built a Temple of Inscriptions, similar to the Egyptian pyramids, to house his remains. He was in a full feather headdress and the lines of the white sculpture were exquisite, classic Mayan, giving it a smooth, flowing impression, like a figure by Zuñiga.

Esmeralda's restaurant was called Antojitos Mayas. It was a three-sided thatched hut with ceiling fans and small wooden tables. Her menu was posted on a blackboard daily and consisted of local Mayan and Mexican fare. The average price of a meal was three dollars, and although I took my meals with her household, this was what I paid her. Chon was right; she was a superb cook. That first night she served us squash soup and shredded wild turkey rolled in blue corn tortillas, covered with a pumpkin seed sauce. After three days of eating tamales from platform vendors, it was a veritable feast.

All Mayan huts have the same form, although their size may vary greatly. The *Yotoch,* as it is called, is bathtub-shaped and has no windows, only a front and back door. The walls are either wattle and daub or whitewashed adobe, and the roof is always a heavy thatch. The inside is cool and dark and, with hammocks strung across strong support beams, very practical. Outside there are often fruit trees, *milpas* (corn fields), fragrant flowering plants, animals, and the kitchen hut, which has a hewn-stone or cement wood-burning stove, a wooden table, and earthenware pots and the like.

Esmeralda's place consisted of a large family hut in the back, a small visitor's hut beside it, a kitchen hut, and, a short walk away, the restaurant. There were avocado and mango trees, red and purple bougainvillea, and a few chickens and turkeys. She had a milpa several miles away. All in all, it was a naturally beautiful locale with a strange dream-like peace.

four

~

My first night sleeping in a hammock in the jungle was an amazing experience. The sensation of near-weightless suspension was very peaceful. A breeze blew through the open doors, gently rocking the hammock. The strangeness of the jungle noises enthralled me. Some were beautiful, including a birdcall that sounded like a pebble plunking into water. Others were supremely distracting; the cicada concert became quite rowdy. And still others were evocative, summoning images of ghosts stalking in the shadows. The howler monkeys were, to say the least, most inconsiderate. Since they sat high in the trees their cries, akin to animal growls or long horn honks, penetrated and blared from everywhere. The cacophony of notes would quiet down for a moment after they yowled, as if the whole jungle was wondering whether they were sounding a predator alert or just mimicking one another. I was completely enchanted by my night in Eden.

In the morning I felt quite refreshed. After I got dressed and stepped out of my hut, I found Esmeralda in an embroidered tunic dress feeding the chickens before she opened the restaurant for breakfast. Her shiny bronze skin glowed with freshly washed softness and her braids were still wet. Jungle Maya bathe many times a day. Chon was scooping fresh water from the rain barrel with a ladle.

"Good morning!" Esmeralda sang to me as she scattered feed and hens clucked at her feet.

"Good morning to you," I replied, walking over to her.

"We'll have breakfast in a little while. There's a bucket if you want to bathe. I spend all day with the people in the restaurant. You're welcome to come and talk with me, but I think Chon would like you to watch his healing work today. See how we do things in this part of the world. Don't worry, you'll get used to the rhythm around here. I'm sure the pace is much slower than you're used to." Esmeralda smiled at me again and pointed in Chon's direction. "You should go and watch him before we eat. He's getting ready to do the count."

I turned and looked at Chon, who had set up a small table and two chairs under a tree. As I wandered over I could see that the tabletop had a checkerboard design with about twenty red and black squares. Chon was seated in one of the chairs.

A heavyset man approached him. "Greetings, Chuch!" the man called out. Chon stood up and the two men shook hands. The man sat down in the chair across from him. I went over and sat on a nearby tree stump to watch. Chon emptied a bag of crystals and coral tree seeds into a pile on the board. "What is it you want to know?" he asked.

"My life isn't going well here," the man said. "I'm wondering if I shouldn't take my wife and move back to Piste where her family is from and abandon this area. Or should I leave her here and take a job as a jungle guide to the ruins of Bonampak, which a friend has offered me? It means that I'll be away most of the time but I'll be able to send money home."

Chon began to group the crystals and seeds into little arrangements within the squares. While making each small pile he mumbled a few words, as if he were counting or praying. It appeared to be some sort of mathematical divination. When he finished Chon looked up at the man. "You should do both," he announced. "Take your wife and children home and leave them with her mother in Piste. They can all live more happily for less, and your wife will be able to care for her mother, who'll soon need it. You may then take the job as a guide until something closer to Piste comes along."

The man was elated and thanked Chon profusely, shaking his hand heartily several times. After the man got up and left, Chon swept the seeds and crystals back into his pouch and motioned for me to accompany him to the kitchen hut. "Let's eat before too many people come," he called to me.

Esmeralda set out fresh pineapple juice, papaya, scrambled eggs with fresh chilies, and tortillas for breakfast. As we ate Chon dabbed the perspiration from his forehead after each bite of chili. "Chilies are very good for your teeth," he told me.

"What was all that business with the seeds?" I asked him as Esmeralda brought out more tortillas.

"Chon is a Chuch Kaháu," Esmeralda said offhandedly. "That means 'lineage head' or 'keeper of the sacred count' in our language. In Tikal, close to where we come from, divinatory calculations were done in ancient times and then kept. While in a Dream state and using the count, Chon is able to answer questions about the future." She glanced at Chon with pride and smiled. "He's never wrong," she added. "He sees into people, their motives, their energy, their designs. You'll witness that today."

I listened respectfully while stuffing my mouth with papaya. Chon and Esmeralda glanced at each other. At that moment Eligio, Tiófilo, and Ignacio showed up and sat down at the table, greeting their mother first, then their uncle and me in an exaggerated way, as if they shared an insider's joke. "So how do you like it here? It's beautiful, isn't it?" Tiófilo asked me. "Yes!" I said eagerly, still stuffing my face. Everyone laughed.

"Thought we'd come say hello before we go off to work," Eligio added.

"What do you do?" I asked, grabbing a tortilla.

"We're guides at the ruins but also work in our fields and hire ourselves out for the excavations," Ignacio told me.

"Have you eaten?" their mother asked.

"Yes, thanks, Mom," they all said in the same exaggerated manner. The three young men accepted cups of coffee instead. I recognized the custom of allowing someone you visit to do something for you, whether you really want it or not.

"Well," Eligio said, brushing off his white tunic shirt and rising politely from the table when they had finished their coffee, "we're going. The ruins open early. I know our uncle is going to take you there himself, but if you need anything from us during your stay please let us know. We're all at your service," he said gallantly. With that pronouncement, they kissed their mother, shook my hand, and grabbed a few tortillas as they went out the door.

Several young Mayan women arrived to start the day's work at the restaurant. They were dressed beautifully in dark blue ruffled cotton skirts and embroidered off-the-shoulder white blouses. Esmeralda went off with them. Chon and I remained seated at the table in the kitchen hut. I felt strangely self-conscious as certain feelings surfaced inside me. I stared down at my food. I must have been blushing.

When I raised my face, Chon was smiling knowingly. "Chuch Kaháu?" I asked him.

This time he turned away. "Yes," he said softly. "You didn't know?" he asked ingenuously, cracking a smile.

"Maybe I did," I mumbled as I nervously chewed on my tortilla.

"We know each other already," Chon assured me as he stood up from the table. "You're a brave girl, Merilyn. When you're finished here come into the curing hut. I'll have patients by then." He calmly strolled off in the direction of the smaller of the two dwelling huts.

Watching Chon's cures that day was incredible. The hut was filled with dense, fragrant copal smoke. He had unpacked and began to use bundle after bundle of medicinal plants. The patients would enter, sit down in a chair across from him, and enumerate their maladies. Chon would sit and gaze at them through the smoke until he "saw their energy." The recommended cures took myriad forms. Some patients were laid on a wooden table covered with a thick straw mat. Then they were massaged with aromatic ointments while Chon recited incantations. Others left with herbs and instructions on how to prepare and administer them, while some were instructed to take baths and/or were put on special diets. People would leave items to be empowered or they would ask Chon to make them little bundles to carry around. I also saw him give people items to bury, place ignited paper cones inside patients' ears, fan smoke over some, and spit corn liquor around the bodies of others.

Another part of Chon, almost like a hypnotic self, often took over and rose through the smoke to touch sparkling or dull places in the patients' energy fields, which could be clearly seen through the hanging copal vapors as a luminous cloud surrounding them. When this happened Chon's breathing would change and become very audible, like air pumping into a bicycle tire. It was as if another body came out of him to heal his patients. The overall effect of this phenomenon was extremely graceful, exotic, and thoroughly mesmerizing.

Chon appeared to have a strong effect on babies, and many mothers came with children who had stopped suckling or cried a lot and did not sleep well. He would slap the babies on their bellies but they never cried, smiling back at him instead. He then massaged their little bodies and rubbed their palms while he cooed Mayan prayers over them. The babies always seemed gleefully animated afterwards, and the mothers left ecstatically happy and thankful.

Payment was varied. There was a cylindrical basket outside the hut where people dropped money, or they would leave fruit, vegetables, candles, incense, chickens—whatever they had and could afford. The length of cure also varied. Some mothers brought their babies back for several visits before they were completely healthy and recovered.

There was one elderly woman who could not walk. Her children carried her to Chon that afternoon for a healing, and she was asked to stay. She ended up sharing the curing hut with me for nine days. After receiving massages and instructions she was able to walk feebly on the third day by holding onto her daughter's arm. By the seventh day she could support herself with a cane, and on the ninth day she was tottering around slowly without any aid.

It was true what his nephews had said about people lining up for the cure. By late afternoon every day, there was a line all the way to the restaurant. When Esmeralda was short on customers she would bring out the metal folding chairs from the restaurant for the people to sit. They could also help themselves to the cool water in the rain barrel.

With all this activity Antojitos Mayas did very good business. It was popular with tourists looking for that "real local" place and for the "real locals." The restaurant was open from eight in the morning until ten at night, and the young Mayan women would work the entire day with alternating lengthy breaks and their three meals. Esmeralda supervised and cooked the food, as well as tending to things at the house and providing support for her brother when needed.

This first afternoon, like those that followed, one of the young women from the restaurant brought our lunch to the kitchen hut. We had chicken lime soup and red and blue corn *gorditas*, corn masa breads shaped into inch-thick ovals and stuffed with various ingredients such as cheese or vegetables and served with assorted sauces. The diverse colors of this dish were very appealing.

After lunch Chon stretched his arms at the table, no doubt tired from his strenuous morning schedule. He had changed into a light blue tunic and a freshly pressed pair of the area's white cotton pants. He now fiddled with one of his jade earplugs. There was a hole about the size of a slender drinking straw in each of his earlobes.

"Where did you get those? They look old," I said, referring to the earrings.

"Oh, a friend of mine found them at a site and gave them to me as payment for a healing. I had to pierce my ears so I could wear them," he remarked casually. He turned to me and in a more serious tone said, "Merilyn, I'm thinking of stopping early today so we'll have the rest of the afternoon for exploring the ruins."

"That sounds great, if you can spare the time," I said eagerly. Then I asked, "How much do you charge as a guide?"

Chon actually shuddered and looked back at me with great patience. "This is not a money arrangement. I thought you understood that. You can invite me and do things for me whenever you like and vice versa. Here," he said and sweetly handed me a flat, dark green stone, "it's a jade. Somebody threw it in the payment basket."

Chon stood up and left to treat the last of his patients

for the day. I sat back in my chair and watched him walk away, pondering his extraordinary offer. Giving me the jade was a superb gesture. I should have been paying him not only for showing me the ruins but also for the rare glimpses into his healing practice, a line of study that now interested me immensely. All this given unconditionally. It made me wonder what strange fate had brought us together.

Later in the afternoon, Chon donned a baseball cap turned backward, picked up his machete, and said it was time to start out for the ruins. We headed into the jungle behind the huts. He hacked his way along a path, staying about a hundred feet ahead of me. The deep green foliage reached out and enveloped us like a desperate lover. After a while we approached a cool, rocky stream. The birds greeted us with a song.

"If we follow the stream down, it'll take us to the ruins behind the Temple of Inscriptions," Chon said, standing next to the rushing, gurgling water. "Going in the other direction would take us to the waterfall. This is the water that the ancient Maya diverted for their underground sewer system."

We tromped down the stony green ground toward the site. The water flowing beside us was cold and bubbling. A sensation of timelessness amid the emerging sunlight was building within me. I began to see a break in the jungle, a clearing, and then . . . the back of a monumental limestone pyramid.

I felt very strange. "Chon," I called out. "Wait." My knees were becoming weak. I was all rubber-legged, which was odd given my superb physical condition. I practically collapsed into a sitting position and instinctively stuck my feet, sandals and all, into the cold stream. I stared hypnotically into the clear flowing water.

Chon crept back up to me stealthily. "Don't go to sleep here," he whispered cryptically. "It's time to wake up." A cricket started singing loudly. Chon tapped my shoulder softly and smiled with concern in his face, removing his cap. He then plucked tamarind seeds from the pod of a resident tree and handed them to me.

"Oh, my God!" I gasped. "It's the dream!" I cried, holding the seeds in my palm and looking up at Chon. My eyes were tearing. Now, for the first time, I was able to "see" him. His face, though middle-aged, had the ancient look of timeless experience. He had taut tan skin, high wide cheekbones. His long and narrow nose was not the classic beak seen in the faces of so many Maya and yet, for a moment, I saw him standing before me in the traditional white tunic of centuries past. I looked away but his dark eyes bored into me with loving intensity. He was the man I had dreamed of on the first night I stayed with don Juan! My body was numb with shock.

"It's all right. Come on," he cooed to me softly, holding out his hand.

I hesitated for a moment, unsure of my willingness or ability to go on, but something shifted in me and I held out my hand. I rose lightly into the air, as if leaving my body's weight below at the water's edge. We walked on, my hand held softly in his, until we reached the site in the shadow of the big temple.

Dazzling light radiated from the edifices. They sputtered with coiled energy in the sunlight, like the tails of rattle-snakes. The baking white limestone rose in stark geometric shapes, reflecting against the dark green rustling jungle. Massive mirages balanced on the colossal scales of architectural perfection. They towered over us, glaring down at us as if they were gods incarnate.

"Do you know who's buried here?" Chon asked, referring to the towering step pyramid, topped with an oblong temple.

"The Temple of the Inscriptions houses the remains of the Aháu Pacal Votán," I expounded, gazing at a hieroglyph from my somnambulistic state. I perceived in my mind's eye a deep tomb and a mosaic jade death mask. "He ruled in the seventh century A.D., the classic period of the kings, before the post-classic rise of the warriors at Chichén Itzá."

"Good!" Chon whispered, tapping my forehead between the brows with his index finger and then pointing to a smaller temple on a far hill with a skyscraping lattice roof comb. "And there?"

"Are housed the remains of his son, Cham Balom," I uttered in a trance, and then added, "which have not been discovered yet." I was taken aback by the certainty of my pronouncement; archaeologists only suspect that Cham Balom is buried there.

Chon smiled. "So!" he affirmed. He pulled me to the palace across from the temple. I stared at its tall watchtower. We entered a low stone doorway and could see the bedchamber. Somehow I knew that the slab would be covered with jaguar furs. Outside the sleeping area I also recognized the steam chamber, a sunken stone room for bathing, with its U-shaped squatting hole, both graced with water flowing underneath.

We strolled into an interior palace courtyard. The four ends had several stairs, each set leading up to columned platforms that were formerly covered by thatched roofs. This palace looked familiar. The reliefs showed a noble in a full woven straw-and-feather headdress sitting cross-legged in one of the four seats of honor, while in the courtyard below other nobles perforated the tips of their large stylized penises. I could almost see him observing them, sitting elegantly in long green quetzal feathers!

Chon sat down cross-legged on the northerly of these platforms and motioned for me to do likewise on the southern platform opposite him. "This ritual," he said, nodding at the reliefs, "was to induce visions." He spoke loudly enough for me to hear him across the short distance of the courtyard. "There is a species of sacred mushroom that has always grown in these parts. On the night of ceremony, the genital or tongue flesh was perforated with thorns or sliced with an obsidian blade. The spattered blood was caught on paper made of fig bark and read for its design, then offered up burnt to the gods. At that moment, powdered mushroom would be pushed into the wound and sniffed through the nostrils or smoked. The fresh mushroom flesh would also be eaten or drunk in a liquid boiled with water and the blood of the participants."

"What type of visions were produced?" I asked, completely entranced.

"Ecstatic visions of deities and their realms and designs. Visions of time, the now, before, and after," Chon responded somberly. "I still collect the mushrooms from around here and perform this ancient ceremony on occasion." He lifted up his shirt and revealed fine line scars on his torso, as if baring his heart. "Someday, I think you will want to participate with me."

The prospect was intriguing. "Is there a Mayan calendar here?" I asked him impulsively. "Not long ago, I dreamed of one in the forest not far from these ruins." I was referring to the stone disk calendar from my dream on the first night with don Juan. "You . . . yes, it was you! You threw tamarind seeds . . ." I opened my pocket and pulled out the seeds given to me earlier. "You threw tamarind seeds on two of the dates." I blinked, stupefied, staring at the seeds again. I felt like I was falling through the center of the earth.

"There are calendars and many calculations, but they're not here. I am, though." Chon said gently. "One calendar is ceremonial and is based on the 260-day cycle of the fetus in the womb. Another calendar is annual and measures time in eighteen groups of twenty days each, with five days of purging at the end of each year. The first calendar is prophetic and runs backward from A.D. 2012 to 3313 B.C.E."

"That's the one I mean!" I called out, feeling that I not only knew something about it, but was intimately connected to it.

"All the calendars were designed a long time ago, and the annual was later adjusted in Xochicalco," he continued, peering at me from across the courtyard. "All of them are still used by Maya today. There were also calculations done on the phases of Venus, which is the light in the heavens that represents Kukulkán and which go backward from the time of the calendars, some fifty million years, and ahead to 2012."

I experienced a momentary vision of the blue light of Venus in the night sky sparkling and becoming the totality of my right eye. "Why does the prophetic calendar stop?" I asked, and then had the eerie realization that I had repeated, almost word for word, this question from my earlier dream.

"That's the part of the mystery—the mystery the mushroom smoke might help you unravel," Chon said.

"Have I been having some kind of prophetic dreams?"

"You could call them that. Or you could say that you have been seeing, remembering, or even awakening."

"How will I know when it's time to try the mushrooms with you?"

"You'll know by your urgent need to understand what's happening to you. It'll be very powerful, more powerful than it has ever been. Even more powerful than it is right now, at this moment," he said, staring off, deep in thought.

I told Chon the story of Richard Morrison and don Juan. He listened attentively while the sky turned scarlet and then purple. Cicadas and night birds began to call. It was winter, and so the jungle was fresh and fragrant at the twilight hour. Chon's eyes had become slits peering into the vastness of the unknown mystery. "He's very wise, that old Indian. There's more to him than meets the eye. As for your lover, I agree with what don Juan told you about him, that he served as a bridge to get you here."

"What's going to happen to me now that I'm here?"

"Marvels. I have counted you," Chon replied solemnly. "It'll be better if we let your designs unfold naturally and I give you guidance as you go along. Just trust in your instinctive power to always do the right thing, in the intent you bring with you to this world, and in your own tremendous energy. Things are going to culminate rather mysteriously." Chon lowered his head again and closed his eyes for a moment, then stood up from his cross-legged position in one fluid movement, brushing himself off. He walked down to the bush level and stepped into the jungle.

It had become quite dark. Chon returned with a torch, crudely fashioned from a thick branch and some dry banana leaves. The light from the flame cast strange shadows on the stones and the reliefs. We withdrew from the palace and walked off the site, our feet mingling with the small moist plants until we reached the trail. Chon said we had better catch the local bus instead of returning through the jungle at night, to avoid the occasional jaguar.

As we waited for the bus in the damp blue-blackness of the night, I asked him, "What would happen if I tried the smoke now?"

He smiled and patted me on the head. "You wouldn't understand it yet," he replied gently. "Not quite yet."

five

~

I was intrigued by Chon's practice of energetic healing and stayed with him, learning and absorbing as much as I could. Over time Chon began to instruct me, which included long talks about what he called the Dream Body or Energy Body. He would have me sit beside him in the smoke, gazing through it. He demonstrated how to "rise up into energy" using a special breath and "third eye" visual focus, and how to walk as if I were floating in order to step through the spiraling smoke and touch sparkles in the energy fields or clouds of the patients. Chon told me that I was prepared for this work because I was naturally endowed with vast amounts of energy, that its use was a form of magic and was to be taken seriously.

"You have already forged an Energy Body. You move energy with it. Heaven knows how you achieved it. Perhaps it's your courage, or perhaps you were born with it," he said with a mysterious inflection one day, after having demonstrated how to slice the energy field of a patient and peel her like a banana. "It takes most people years of tedious labor to access, extract, and move energy, along with exercises in Dreaming, which seem to be second nature to you. You intuitively understand everything. It is as if you are able to reach the center of the universe. This should be the natural state of all human consciousness, but unfortunately it has been diluted. Even seeing energy directly is almost impossible for most people.

"Once the Energy Body is accessed, you gradually start transferring more and more energy to it, *distilling,* as it were, your physical existence, your metaphors and symbols, your feelings and consciousness, sending them to reside in energy, in the Creative Dream. You offer them up, abstracted, concentrated, and alchemized, and breathe fire into them. This leads to the ability to enter into pure energy with the body.

"Most people want to control everything with their minds, which prevents the possibility of their ever leaving the energetic realm of dissection/recreation with their identities intact to enter into the eternal realm of pure wholes and of healing. They'll think they've crossed a threshold, broken through a barrier, but what really happens is that they've expanded the mind and are hoarding more there.

Some even swim in delusion. There are those who visualize everything but never take the body, so their knowledge is nearly useless in a crunch. These people lose almost everything in death because they never truly moved into energy in life.

"This isn't the case for you. I'm obliged to tell you what to do now. There are four ways to effectively transfer everything, or almost everything, to energy." Chon sat down on his wooden chair in the curing hut, and I sat against the wall facing him. I had never seen him so gravely serious. "The first two deal with consciousness transference. Through a sunlike explosion of one's energy or through a shimmering rainbow, all awareness is moved to the Dream Body once it is forged. This transfer leaves the physical body behind as a hollow, completely empty shell. The being now inhabits the spiritualized Energy Body permanently.

"The latter two ways actually transmute or transfigure the cellular structure with golden fire within energy or the ascending rainbow. One takes everything and literally walks into heaven with all one has, body and all. One passes through fire and water. These are four ancient practices. Everything else is a spin-off. Or even a delving into levels of death, or a digression into freezing time.

"Every now and again," Chon continued as he chopped wild yam with a machete on a tree stump in front of his chair, "people will come to you for healings who are already partially dead and don't realize it. They have experienced a level of death in spirit or energy, often in a realm of slower vibration, as the result of witchcraft or of their own susceptibilities. You will feel yourself gear down when their energy appears before you. Time will stretch."

I gasped and put my hand in front of my mouth.

He stopped chopping and glared at me. "People who're going to heal or resurrect must be able to look upon death," he said soberly. "You'll enter into the energy with your body. There's someone I want you to see. Once you lay eyes on him you'll understand what I'm talking about. He's one of these living dead. Several years ago he fell prey to some witches and wizards in San Andres Tuxtla and is now trapped in the inorganic or preorganic realm with forces that possess unusual powers but can only go so far. I've personally tried and then tried with others to pull him out of it but so far all our attempts have failed. I think he'll like you, or like your energy. Perhaps he'll let you awaken him to what has happened and follow you out. That would bring about a healing for him.

"In any case, this type of healing is accompanied by deep symbolic seeing, which you have the visionary capacity to engage. Since you have so much natural energy you'll find yourself slipping into this other realm bodily even before you see him, but once you actually make contact, once you're there, your mind won't function normally. You won't be able to think about what you're doing. You'll just do it." Chon made a spiral gesture around the left side of his head, seemingly to indicate that the left brain would shut off. "You'll have to trust your innate symbolic understanding and have the courage to perform whatever that requires. It's a leap of faith and it requires tremendous courage. No counting of cost. It's the only means of moving energies in these realms."

I was very concerned, terribly unsettled. This was much deeper work than the healings in the hut, but Chon assured me that my facility to Dream and his guidance would make it possible and that this next level would connect me to my ability to "cross over." From the beginning Chon had been telling me to observe the energetic practices of individuals I saw at the herbalists' market in the Tuxtlas. This area was pervaded with dark flying shadows and had a cocooned or even embalmed, deathlike quality. And the surrounding hills were always covered with mist.

"There is one warning. In crossing into an inorganic realm you'll also realize that it's possible for forces there to cross into this realm. Some will try to latch on to you in order to follow you out. This, of course, is a goal of sorcery, to work with these forces and encourage them to manifest. Healers learn to deal with them by necessity."

Chon sensed my agitation. At his suggestion, we walked to the stream below the waterfall so I could gaze into the water and attempt energetic contact with this individual he called Coyol. "Feel yourself traveling the waterways of the underworld," he whispered in my ear. "Let the waters take you to him."

I knew that if Chon was worried this task must be pretty dreadful. He seemed to care about Coyol very much. Trying to center myself, I sat on a cool slippery rock, staring into the rushing water and slowly becoming mesmerized by it. The sky was gray and so the water had a silvery glow. I felt myself rushing, first inside my body as blood and then with a flash of energy I transferred my awareness outside my body to the water extending into the tributaries and rivers of the earth. After some time I felt a shock as my awareness collected. Some part of me was gazing on the dead body of a small robust man with dark wavy hair, floating face down. I cried out desperately and pulled myself back from this vision. I shook my head frantically. "Oh, no, Chon!" I wept. "Oh, no!"

As we journeyed to San Andres, we did Entry Dreaming, as Chon called it. This Dreaming differs from the spiral Dreaming of don Juan, which pulls out of the uncreated, in that this process is the reverse; it bores into the realms of energy. It shifted me into my Dream Body.

The bus to San Andres Tuxtla is small and old. We sit on uncomfortable seats and view the road winding through the foggy hillsides. The mist is a Dream Barrier of some sort, almost like a veil that will not lift, a Dream Spell. When we finally arrive and step off the bus, we have passed through it. The people in the plaza are moving silently in their colorful clothes, like shadows or ghosts. A light rain is falling, almost like tears.

Chon secures a double room for us in a modest Mexican pension. We sit in the inner courtyard that evening, roasting corn and yams on a small charcoal grill. The world around us seems to evaporate in the smoke, as though it exists only where we fix our attention. We walk like somnambulists to our room and fall asleep under coarse blankets and dim kerosene light.

In the morning Chon manifests, seemingly out of nowhere, a blouse and full skirt of the simple style worn by the women of this hill region. The skirt is a pink cotton print covered with large green butterflies. The button-down blouse is the same rosy pink. This outfit magically speaks to me of transformation. I bathe with a bucket of water and braid my hair while Chon heats tamales on the grill. Afterwards we walk slowly to the marketplace.

Chon does not have to point Coyol out to me. My eyes shift straight to him when we arrive at the entrance to the market building. He is maybe five foot four and is in his fifties, very robust with short, dark wavy hair. There is an older woman standing with him selling fruits and herbs. He is helping her but she appears to be holding him back, as if her "heaviness" weighs upon him, making his life impossible.

"You're already sensing intuitively. Just observe and let yourself go into it," Chon whispers in my ear as we stand across the street

from them. "Remember, you are stepping into his energy and this is a slower vibrational realm. It is energy; it is not the realm of daily life, no matter how it may appear. Feel the empathy inside you and let it pull you to them. Remember, your mind will not operate here, only your symbols, actions, and feelings. You may not even be able to speak at first. Act instinctively but with a higher purpose."

I observe that the older woman treats Coyol as a slave, almost as if he were retarded and she were exploiting him. His heavy body lumbers under the crates he is moving for her. Just then, from around the corner, comes Esmeralda with about seven little children scurrying behind her! I shake my head in disbelief. What is Esmeralda doing here? Chon reads my thoughts. "She is doing the same as you. Watch her magic!" he says with obvious admiration. "She too brings almost everything with her. By contrast, look at Coyol. In the first world, or that of ordinary reality, he's very bright and has great power and influence, but none of that is transferable to this realm—it's too mental, too material. Here he is a shadow of himself!"

I find that I cannot form a real thought or mentally react to this scene. All I can do is watch Esmeralda. The little children now call out to Coyol. "Caballo! [horse] Caballo!" They jump with glee. "Caballo! Caballo!" He spins around and grins at them, and they gallop around him trying to hop on his back. Their laughter sounds like joyful music at the water's edge. Esmeralda herds the children into a spiral around Coyol. Then they enter the market and there is *a little puff of smoke, as she and the children disappear through the shadowy opening. This scene unravels like a dream! I shake my head again, trying to believe what I have just seen.*

The old woman tries to lure "Caballo" back to work, but he spots me standing across the street with Chon and will not budge. Chon bids me to cross the energetic barrier between us and Coyol and then disappears around a corner. I am all alone in this venture. I gulp down the lump in my throat and take a few steps toward Coyol. I feel a strong, almost gravitational force pulling me through some kind of vortex into a heavier, slower, darker place. Chon is right. This world is not as it appears on the surface.

At first Coyol stares at me bold-faced as I make my entrance. Then he turns and watches me out of the corner of his eye as I cross the street and approach a glass case filled with handmade lace, which is inside the market but to the right of the old woman. When I turn around to look back at him he has stepped over and is standing right behind me, his staring face practically touching mine.

I take a deep breath. I have crossed the barrier between life and death. Coyol's face is sad and curious at the same time. His eyes are watery and murky brown but have a strange silvery light, especially the left one. The old woman nudges him in the ribs and pushes him out of the way. "Such a pretty young girl!" She is wearing a black and gray rebozo over her head and shoulders and is otherwise dressed in black. She stands taller than Coyol and has a weathered face.

I cringe. For a moment I am mute. There is a heavy sleep-state

energy emanating from this old woman. She is obviously a power-
ful witch.

"Would you like to buy some of my fruit or herbs? I have lots of
yummy treats for a lovely girl like you." She points a strong hand
to an ample array of tropical fruits, the most beautiful being glossy
purple zapote, which tastes like the filling of pecan pie.

I shake my head in slow motion. It takes a great exertion on my
part just to respond. "I'm with that man over there." I point to
Chon, who has reappeared across the street and is watching me care-
fully. "He told me not to buy anything," I say, as innocently as a
child.

The old woman sees that she has been exposed and is angry at
first. "Young girls like you should learn from an old woman like
me." She casts me an engaging glance.

"With all due respect," I retort, now strengthening, "I'm sure
there's much I could learn from you, but we're going to be here only
a short time." Chon grins at me from across the street and then
steps into a shop.

The old woman looks astonished. "I won't hurt you. You're too
strong. But you could learn a lot from me. Why don't you think
about it. We could make some good trades." She ambles back to her
fruit stand and sits down.

I see my chance. "I will consider it, if you'll let me borrow your
helper for a while."

Her eyes flare and then she glances at Coyol scornfully, as if he
were a dumb beast. "Him? Oh, he won't do you any good, but I'll

let him walk you around the market if you promise to bring him back."

I nod my head. Coyol and I walk into the dark market entrance. He points to a vendor who has fresh lemonade in a large glass jug called a garafón. He anxiously jingles change in his loose pants pockets. He wants to buy me a glass. I accept the offer, and he proudly hands me my lemonade while buying one for himself. We lean against a dark wall to drink. He is ogling me the whole time.

A dark young fellow of about twenty walks past us, leering at me. Coyol casually sticks out his right foot and trips the man, who loses his predatory expression in his embarrassment. I grin at the suppressed humor on Coyol's face.

"Where do I know you from?" he asks in a voice neither high nor deep.

I answer with a pleading glance, remembering how I saw him floating dead in the "spirit waters."

"I'm serious!" he insists emphatically.

"I saw you dead," I finally say.

He shakes his head in bewildered shock. "Ah!" he says.

With a furrowed brow "Caballo" takes our glasses back and anxiously motions for me to follow him out a side entrance of the market and down a small street. I walk behind him the entire way, his pace is so quick. When we arrive at his dwelling place I am horrified. There is a barred gate leading into a small, dusty alleyway. Standing alone in the dirt is a minute cement construction, no larger than an oversized walk-in closet with a roof. A whirlwind is scattering blank sheets of paper in a spiral above and around the tiny cell.

We step inside. There are no furnishings, nor is there any room for them. There is only a mattress and several large plastic jars in a corner, filled to the brim with coins. Outside, there is a water spigot. Coyol stands in the shadows beside the closed, low wooden door.

"Can I see you?" he asks, referring to my body by making gestures of disrobing.

My heart goes out to him. His life here is so sad and he barely realizes his predicament. I sense, relying on my intuitive powers, that the only way to show him the difference between real life and his death-sleep is to honor his request and reveal my body to him. I gracefully take off my clothes and stand naked before him. A whooshing sound escapes his lips, as he peers at me from the shadows.

He now motions for me to lie down on the mattress. I do so without hesitation, flowing with the feeling of appropriate response. He undresses himself. His brown body is rather nice, with full and rounded muscles and buttocks. He lies down beside me, I on my left side, he on his right. We just gaze at each other. Then he moves closer so that we are almost but not quite touching everywhere.

"I'm dead?" he asks me pitifully.

"Yes," I tell him somberly, filled with longing for his lost life, for him.

"*They told me you were coming. Can't you feel anything?*" *he asks, referring to himself.*

"*Yes, I feel you,*" *I say.* "*I care about you. Come with me.*"

"*Where?*" *he asks, looking frantic.*

"*Out there, away from this,*" *I say and gesture spatially to him.*

"*No, please. You stay here with me,*" *he pleads with me.*

My heart is breaking. He does not realize that I love him and that he can trust me fully. Why do I have such feelings for him? I do not think about it, just feel it deeply. Perhaps the universe is loving him through me and redeeming some small part of itself in the process. I can feel everything about him, that he considers himself ugly, but to me, in this moment, he is the most beautiful man alive. He also sees himself as dull, uninspired, and partially complete, which is pain foisted upon him. His mind and spirit are keen, almost brilliant, I sense. My whole body aches for him, especially my heart, which pangs and wants to burst out of my chest. I start to weep.

"*Don't cry for me,*" *he says softly.*

"*Please, please come with me,*" *I beg him.*

"*I'll never make it,*" *he mumbles, shaking his head sorrowfully.*

I become desperate. "*Please, you can't stay here,*" *I entreat him, watching the spinning shadows forming around the room.* "*You've got to come!*"

"*I can't,*" *he concedes as somberly as death itself.*

"*I'll come back for you then. I promise! I swear it! I'll come back! But you must go back to the market. I can't leave you here with all these flying shadows.*"

"They're the powers the witches and wizards use to control this place," he says furtively, as if he were avoiding the flight of bats.

Coyol and I dress dutifully, and I walk with him down the small street back to the old woman at the market. He returns to her service almost as if he were a zombie, but he watches me out of the corners of his eyes, and I sense his longing. Just then, one of the shadows approaches me and suddenly coagulates, right before my eyes, into a small white-haired man. I can see that energetically it is not human but one of the inorganic or preorganic forces Chon told me about.

"What are you going to do now?" it asks me.

I shake my head and shrug my shoulders in confusion. The shadow motions for me to touch it lightly on the hand and when I do we spin slowly, losing track of our physical location, until I am standing at the bus station with Chon.

I walk toward Chon as if hypnotized. He makes a spiraling movement with his arms and points a small distance away from me. Stepping off a bus is a spidery little man with grayish-white hair and a sad face. I do a double take and peer deeply into the face. My God! It's Coyol! Old, sad, and serious. Lost, drained, and alone.

I run out of there without thinking, heading back to the market. My heart is pounding, my breath rasping. I hurl myself and it starts to rain. It is raining, Merilyn, I tell myself. It is raining! No! No! I get to a muddy corner of the marketplace and see Coyol standing there, still young, but we are separated by the energy barrier. It is like peering through a sheet of water or thick *window glass. All the colors begin to bleed. Drops of blue and green, like little teardrop-earths seen from space. He crouches against the old building, unprotected, alone on the other side of the barrier to hide his tousled head from the water. Chon comes from out of nowhere and gently touches my shoulder. It is time to leave. Coyol has not come out.*

six

~

While I am in this vulnerable state, Chon escorts me back to the bus station, explaining that I am still in my Dream Body. He reveals that it was indeed Esmeralda at the market performing the actions that I witnessed. She and he were also in their Dream Bodies and continue to be so. He informs me that Esmeralda is not his sister but his colleague. All of them, including his three nephews—who are actually his apprentices—are connected to a group of wizards led by don Juan. However, Tiófilo and Ignacio are not as advanced and have remained behind with Eligio in Palenque to continue their tasks of collecting and preparing his medicinal plants.

If Chon were not so exceedingly kind to me I would not trust him so completely. I want to run out of there screaming. I sit on a wooden bench in the corner and shake.

"I know we tricked you." Chon soothes me as he strokes my

hair, "*but it isn't easy to lure people into the wizard's world.*"

"*The two of you didn't kill Richard with your magic?*" *I shriek, horrified.*

"*No, we wouldn't do that, although there're those who would. You could say that he sacrificed himself for you, so you can fulfill your destiny. You're going to do something special, Merilyn, and it begins now.*"

Chon tells me that don Juan has already "*crossed over*" *into a realm of higher energetic vibration, a realm of pure wholes and of healing, and that he'll be waiting for us on the other side of yet a second energetic barrier.* "*This is the place we were trying to take Coyol,*" *he explains.* "*If you had gotten him out I would've led both of you.*" *He begins to explain this process called* "*crossing over*" *and its purpose.*

"*We're going to go through another barrier, like the one you detected between you and Coyol at the market. Only this one will be of a higher vibration. We'll be opening the way for others—perhaps many, who will come after us. We'll go to a lake, a launching point, near the village of Catemaco. We'll go into spiral Dreaming together and one by one we'll step toward the water. A shimmering vortex will appear and we'll step through it and across the water, as if we were walking upon it, walking upon energy. We'll not be the first who've crossed over to this state. Many ancient beings from this land have entered from that very spot.*"

I feel this has always been my destiny. I sense that this is the beginning of the end of death. "*What about Coyol?*" *I wail, teary-eyed.*

Chon's face shatters like an old clay pot. "We've failed to free him; he doesn't have sufficient energy to follow us, at least not for now." His eyes are also visibly tearing. He looks away for a moment.

"What will the vortex be like?" I ask him, trying to overcome my oppressive grief over leaving Coyol behind.

"It will shimmer. As you step across, you'll begin to dissolve. After that it's hard to say what will happen. Just trust power." He speaks with his head still turned away. His shoulders tremble just a little.

"I feel that there's still so much I don't know," I say, lamenting my inexperience.

"There is," Chon remarks soberly. "But this crossing is necessary; necessary for you and for others, and it must happen now. Don't worry, you have a natural facility for it."

"Will I see Richard?" I ask naively.

"No. You'll see other beings, the Ancients, who've crossed over before us."

I delve into my feelings about this extraordinary development on the bus ride to nearby Catemaco. Here we again rent rooms and remain for what seems to be a week but, for all I know could be eons in the first world. We Dream the Entry and the Manifesting Spiral shown to me by don Juan. Catemaco itself is more like a dream world than a real town. It is just an illusory island in the vastness, even less tangible than San Andres.

At a certain moment Chon and I witness two ancient beings dressed in the Indian clothing of these hills but made of colored satins. *They canoe across the enchanted lagoon and step out to wander the lakeside market. A rippling of energy now appears over the lake.*

The two native people, a man who appears to be in his fifties with shoulder-length black hair worn behind his ears, exposing one earring, and a woman with gray braids and a festival-pink satin dress, start to glow more golden. They now turn to gaze at us from a ribbon stand. A breeze blows the multicolored strands of ribbons.

Chon and I walk slowly toward the banks of the lake. I feel a crack literally split open in the air in front of me. There is total silence. My ears do not even have the sensation of deafness. I start to see beings from another world coming through the crack, across the lake, in more white and golden canoes. Chon tells me that these are older wizards who have already crossed and that some of them were his mentors.

Chon steps closer to the water. Time appears to stop. I observe that the people around us are slowing down, as if frozen in the moment. It is certain that they will be unable to see what is about to happen. Chon steps forward and disappears. He shimmers and dissolves as if in water, right before my eyes. Then Esmeralda, out of nowhere, comes walking across the lake holding hands with an older female, both of them becoming younger and more beautiful with each step. Esmeralda's braids have grown to the ground. She and the older woman step past me and there is a "ha" sound, as if Esmeralda were drawing her first breath.

I take a step and enter into a breathless state of eternity. My feet begin to dissolve as if I were walking on the water. Everything glistens. The Ancient Ones, all bearing the marks of their own energies, stand silently along the side like sentries to bid us welcome. Energy rushes from the crack like a river. Behind me I sense unknown beings from other dimensions who cross after me. Then I think of Coyol, that he was left behind, and my heart aches. All of a sudden I feel a great rift, a giant tear like an abyss behind me.

I see don Juan. He is standing above another abyss that has opened in front of me. Lightning is striking there and a huge wind is howling behind him. The edge of this abyss is like a cliff illuminated by an eerie white light, which casts long shadows into the deep crevice.

"Cross again, Merilyn." A bridge appears across the chasm. "You must or you'll have to go back," his voice howls above the wind.

"I can't cross, don Juan!"

"Part of you already has. You must," don Juan shouts.

"I can't! What about Coyol?"

"Then jump," he moans. "I won't lose you! Jump into the abyss and I'll follow!"

"What's going to happen?" I cry out.

"We're going to wander in a nether realm until we come out."

I do not have a choice. I cannot go backward or forward. I step off the edge of the abyss and plummet feet first in total blackness for what feels like an eternity. Don Juan then jumps after me. I do not know how long we wander, but I eventually do reemerge.

When I return I find myself alone in our hotel room in Catemaco, but don Juan, Chon, and Esmeralda are nowhere to be found. My passport is missing from the dresser drawer. All my clothes are gone, except the ones on my back, and even my shoes have disappeared from my feet!

I venture outside into the streets and wander like a phantom, lost. I am totally disjointed. I do not have complete control over my body; just walking steadily is a feat. I try to speak but at first people cannot hear me. It is as if I were a ghost to them. I wonder where Chon and Esmeralda have gone. Chon has apparently left this realm. I weep, but nobody notices. I ask for enough money for the short bus ride to San Andres to search for Coyol. Surely he is still there.

When I arrive in San Andres and go to the market, I do not find Coyol there. How much time has passed? Years? A dark heavy energy like a predatorial spacecraft begins descending around me. A massive shadow transforms into an immense man with curly chestnut hair, who is wearing bronze-colored slacks and a shirt. He appears, walking through the smoke of an entryway and spiraling his arms hurriedly. He motions with emphatic authority for me to sit down on the ground outside the market building. He sits on the spot beside me.

"Where is that man the children call Caballo?" I ask him, crying and wiping my face. "I'm told he works every day outside the market."

This man peers at me forcefully. For some reason, I cannot focus fully on his features. "He is not here! He has gone," he says ferociously.

"Gone?" I screech looking around wildly.

"You've got to go!" he yells at me.

"Where? How?" I plead with him.

"Go! Go! Go!" he shouts, pounding his fist on his knee. "You are in danger here! Where are you from?"

I wail. He stands and disappears into the smoke, walking back through the dark entryway. I stand up as the smoke clears and look around the marketplace. Has his energy shifted me, or is it the world that has shifted? It appears more substantial. Night falls, but I have nowhere to sleep. I crouch outside the market building in the dark, wondering if I am trapped here forever, a wandering ghost in a netherworld.

As the sun rises, I continue to search the streets looking for Coyol. My skirt and blouse are dirty from having spent the night on the ground. As the street vendors set out their wares, I browse the stands of flowers and medicinal herbs, shoes, clothes—-everything you can imagine—asking for work. I offer my services to a woman food vendor setting up for breakfast, but either she cannot hear me well or she is not taking me seriously. I try to convince others how desperately I need a job. I tell them that I have been stranded without money and need bus fare to the Mexican border. I tell them that I will do anything, as long as it is honest work, to raise the fare.

No one seems to understand me and I am very discouraged. I wonder if I will ever get back home. If I tried to call someone would anyone be there? What would I say? I search for a pay phone. The only one in town is on a corner outside the market, but it is dead. I think of Coyol's plight and I feel just as lost. But, unlike him, I might still have a chance.

Dejected, I walk out of the marketplace down a side street. I try to remember the location of Coyol's dwelling, tracing my steps from the day I followed him there. As I turn the corner onto a small street I come upon a person performing for an invisible audience. I have an eerie feeling about this man but let it pass.

Coyol's place is much farther down the street than I remember. The small, dusty thoroughfare stretches out for quite a distance. I decide to keep walking, although the eerie feeling stays with me. I approach a street corner and spy the barred gate between the two old buildings that lead to his place. As I walk across the street I spot a brawny working-class man with shaggy black hair coming out from behind a building. He has a bronze complexion and is wearing dirty brown denim pants, a faded cotton shirt, and a straw hat. He seems lost, however, out of his element, as though he were a stranger to life. He also looks drunk and is wobbling as he walks. His demeanor raises my level of concern, but I feel his pain and am driven by it. I walk up to ask about Coyol. As I approach I sense a dark shadow around him. He stumbles into the alleyway through the barred gate.

"Do you know the man who lives back there?" I call after him, pointing to the small cement structure standing in the dust.

"Ay, you capitalist bitch!" he mumbles blearily, staggering against the building.

"No! I'm not like that . . ." My heart jumps into my throat and I start to back away. I had better get out of here! There is no one else on the street. I guess that he may be a disenfranchised demon.

"Hey!" he yells. "Hey, gringa!" His screams follow me like a death song. He does not let up as I back away. I turn around to recross the street. I feel sweat forming at my temples and on my palms, and I take yet another step away from the gate, keeping my eyes straight ahead. Then I hear a solemn click. He rushes out and grabs my arm from the back. There is hot breath on the crown of my head and a pounding in my ears as he draws next to me, wrenching my arm and pushing the tip of a pistol against my side.

He pulls me into the alleyway. He seems to have taken the place over. What has happened to Coyol? He closes the barred gate across the narrow passage between the two buildings. The alley now appears to be used as a small dumping ground. He drags me farther and pushes me inside the tiny structure, closing the door.

I fall onto the ground. With no windows the place is dark and musty. He lights an oil lamp and hangs it from the rafter. I see the now-stained, bare mattress to my right, with some empty cans, dried tortilla pieces, and fruit peels lying around it. Near them, I spot what looks like a bloody rag on the floor and gasp. Coyol's large plastic jars filled with coins are gone.

"Don't even think about screaming," he says as I grope around on the floor. "Who do you think you are, talking to me like that?" he growls.

"I didn't mean to offend you," I plead, terrified, my eyes adjusting to the dim light. "I wondered if you were all right!"

"Get up! Stand up!" he snarls. The man is sitting down on a wooden crate, rocking, still holding onto the pistol.

I do as he says, but he points the barrel of the gun at my chest, dead center.

"Take off your clothes." He is glaring at me with frozen, icy eyes.

I am horrified as I realize what is happening to me. I begin to unbutton my pink cotton blouse and reveal my braless torso. My modest breasts look very vulnerable in this cement hovel. I unzip my butterfly skirt and slide it down.

When I am completely undressed, with my clothes in a

pile on the floor, this man pushes me onto the filthy mattress. I lie there while he removes his pants, using only one hand and never letting go of the large pistol. I gasp as his pants come off. He falls on top of me, putting the pistol to my head. I tell myself it could be worse. The important thing is for him not to kill me.

I wince in horror, turning my face slightly away. He smells strongly of alcohol and body odor. I brace myself but the rape is over almost as quickly as it begins. Only the slimy feeling remains. There is just a momentary relief. I feel the ordeal is not yet over. However, he does roll off me, turning his back to sit at the edge of the mattress and light a cigarette, placing the matchbook on his bare thigh. I wonder if he will kill me next.

The smell of smoke fills this darkened chamber. Shadows are whirling around like phantoms. He stands up and glowers at me. "If I ever see you around here again I'll kill you," he says with bone-chilling certainty.

I sit silently. "Why?" I wonder to myself.

"And don't dare tell anyone about me being here," he says menacingly, taking a long drag from his cigarette. "No one can know about me. Now get dressed," he spits out, suddenly disgusted by my nudity.

I scramble to gather my clothes, trying to control my trembling as I slip into them. Is it possible that he will let me out of here without further harm? I dress, glancing at him for some sign of hope. His eyes are watery. His face and naked body are dead with anger.

I stand there in hell, taking deep pounding breaths. My energy coils, waiting for an opening. I watch each moment, not knowing what I will do until I do it.

"Get out," he says dully. I spring for the door and race through the alleyway to the gate that, unbelievably, is hanging partially open. I hear a pistol shot in the background and I wonder if he has changed his mind and is now shooting at me. I run with wild, uncontrollable fury. I do not look back until I reach a small intersection about a quarter mile away. There I spot the elderly woman from the market standing on the corner of the next block. I stop in my tracks. She is leering at me from under her black rebozo, as though she is ready to devour me. I feel that I have fallen into a trap; the rape was merely the first step. A truck now pulls up to the stop. I open the door and jump inside, desperately recounting my experience to the simple middle-aged farmer. The driver is very humble and modest, quite shy. He lowers his eyes with shame as I speak. The man is from a neighboring village and is heading back. He offers to drive me there. I thank him profusely.

As we drive away I anxiously look back down the street. The man is not chasing after me. Then, as we pass the old woman on the street, the truck stalls. Several younger women come out of a low building and stand behind her. They now take a few steps toward the truck. I gaze back into the old woman's sleep-inducing stare, and then the truck starts. She gazes imploringly at me as we continue down the dusty road toward the hilly edge of San Andres.

That night, asleep in the truck outside the wattle-and-daub hut of this man and his family, I fall into a Dream.

I Dream of the naked demon in a dark, dank cell. He laughs maniacally, crazed and dangerous. The entity possessing him is accursed, a prisoner of the ancient wizards' underworld. He bellows that transformation is never possible beyond the predatorial death realm. So he enslaves there, and he takes prisoners, seeks energy, and sacrifices.

When I awoke the next morning in this little village and walked around begging for money for bus fare to Mexico City, I found that I had shifted more into the world of ordinary reality. But I realized that I had not, nor ever would, return fully. I was now destined to live with a foot in both worlds, to walk the border between them, slipping in and out.

When I finally arrived at the bus station in Mexico City and walked for miles, barefoot, to the American Embassy, they provided me with a letter, indicating that my passport and tourist papers had been stolen. They also gave me thirty-five dollars for fare on a second-class bus to the border. I picked the one that went to San Luis Rio Colorado on the Arizona border, hoping to find don Juan again. He shouted to me as I plummeted into the abyss that he would not lose me! He jumped with me! Perhaps he had returned to this world. He was my one last hope; if he was not there, my life was irredeemable.

The local bus from the border pulled into Yuma early in
the morning, and I walked straight to the reservation. I
was terrified at the prospect of what I might or might not
find. Unbelievably, don Juan was at his house and had apparently been awaiting my arrival. The front door was open,
and I burst into his clapboard shack. Upon seeing him I
was unable to speak. Don Juan was standing at a gas burner
frying fish in a pan. The smell was quite strong. His body
was taut and his demeanor very serious. He turned his head
and rocked me with a penetrating, imperious look. I felt
that I was going to faint at any moment. Don Juan stepped
over and placed two plates of fish on his small wooden
table and forcefully motioned for me to sit down before I
fell down.

His stare conveyed volumes but I dared not read them. I

felt that don Juan was beginning to work his medicine on me. I soon found that I could not formulate clear thoughts. What was happening to me? The implications of my recent experience were beyond my capacity to comprehend. How could any of this have transpired? I could not eat the fish, whose eyes looked up at me as blankly as death. I walked over and sat silently on the bunk that don Juan kept for my visits and vacantly stared through the open back door with my hands between my knees.

The desert was absolutely still. The sun shone through the wooden slat window at the foot of my bunk. In total shock I became mesmerized and completely absorbed in an array of floating dust particles sparkling in the sunlight. Don Juan walked past, stooping slightly to exit the doorway. He returned a moment later carrying a huge bundle of arrow weed. Setting it down, don Juan filled two drinking gourds with water and took some deer jerky from one of his storage chests. He stepped over and handed me the gourds, which I strapped to my back. I followed him outside.

I knew where we were headed. It was about a five-mile hike into the desert to the pair of sandstone pillars that could be seen against the horizon. We did not talk, which was a welcome relief, nor did we stop to rest along the way. I found that the intense physical exertion and the expansive vista of the desert was very centering. Slowly I began to release the memory of everything that had happened to me.

When we arrived at the designated spot, don Juan made a gesture that commanded total silence. He dug a pit in the soft sand with a large shell scoop he carried with him. He next placed dry mesquite branches from the chaparral in the pit and started a fire. While the mesquite was burning, don Juan unwrapped the bundle of arrow weed. The plants were very long and hardy. He loosely wove some of them into a kind of mat or thatch. After the mesquite had turned to embers, he placed the rest of the loose arrow weed in the pit on top of them.

The plants began to smolder. He placed more and more of them on the fire until they reached the top of the shallow pit. Don Juan then laid the mat of arrow weed over it and motioned for me to lie upon it. I removed the gourds from my back and did what I was told. The pit under me extended from my knees to my shoulders and was a little narrower than the width of my body. I sank down slightly when I lay on the mat but the arrow weed broke my fall before I touched the hot embers. Smoke was everywhere.

"Breathe in the smoke. No matter how much you cough," don Juan told me.

The pit was very hot. Sweat was pouring off me, but I did not cough.

"I'm going to perform a rite for raising the dead. You're dead, whether you realize it or not. You've not come back fully. This is what happened to your spirit. The rite is for calling the spirit and healing the body from the entrapment of the underworld you've just passed through. I'll call back ancient memories in you but they won't surface fully until much later. While you're waiting, you'll be asleep. The memories will come from other levels of awareness and will portray the mysterious struggle between life and death. No matter what you see you must struggle, against all odds, not to give in to them. Knowledge will come to you from the horrors and beauties that are our ancient practices. These memories will begin to resurface in dreams, and if you awaken them you'll be awakened."

Don Juan began to drone a chant and beat on one of the water gourds. He spoke a language I had never heard him speak.

Suddenly, I am losing consciousness from the heat, the smoke, the chanting. My head tosses frantically from side to side. As don Juan chants, visual distortions force their way through the smoke. It is as though a beam of light were descending into the haze. Above that beam is a spinning, howling, golden disk of sunlight. Don Juan's aquiline features stand out against the smoke, becoming sharper and sharper through the light, until it hurts my eyes to look at him. I feel my cells are going to burst with the pressure of the pulsing heat and of his drumming, ever sharper, more intense. The result is an unbearable tension. A high-pitched frequency emitted from the energy is piercing my brain and penetrating every pore of my being.

Don Juan cries out like a wild animal. There is a flash of light and the smoke lifts!

I later realized that the pit had cooled and twilight was approaching. I must have been out of my body, unconscious for a long time. Don Juan motioned for me to rise from the pit. I stood up and drank aggressively from a gourd. He quickly snatched it from my hands and indicated that I should sit on a nearby boulder while he covered over the fire.

We walked deeper into the desert. It was dark when we arrived at the sandstone pillars. Don Juan motioned for us to sit between them for a time to replenish our energy. The pillars themselves rose like a tuning fork out of the crystal-strewn area of craggy desert. Beyond them, as if within a magical pass, were volcanic hills and their mysterious lake.

As the stillness of the night settled in more deeply don Juan took the opportunity to whisper a few words. "It's now necessary to break the bonds of death. All creation needs this release."

I intuitively realized that my ordeal was not entirely about me but rather about death itself. While we sat between the sandstone obelisks a beautiful full moon rose over the horizon. I could feel the pull of this celestial body, and I leaned upright against the pillar to expose more of myself to it. Its reflection appeared in the lake and I released myself into the water to commingle with it. Later don Juan sensed pumas in the area, and we cautiously walked back to his house in the dark.

We arrived back early the next morning. It was still dark and we both slept until noon. When I awoke, don Juan had some corn mush prepared for us. "There's no way to talk about this," he said haltingly. "We're in the flow. What we have to do is navigate it. All of the energies are now in play." We hurriedly headed for the banks of the Colorado. On this trip we brought dried fruits and more water gourds. When we arrived, don Juan unrolled a straw mat and laid it among the reeds and high grasses where we sat close to the flowing water.

"There's a second practice I'm going to share here at the river's edge. It is ancient, older than the pyramids. It was once shared with me. Now it has become my power and my destiny. It is practiced only by the water, on a clear sunny day like today. Otherwise, one obtains a lesser result.

"But first I want to engage you in a physical prayer known as Smoking Skull. It's been used by seers as far back as the beginning. You'll need its wisdom. I want you to see the glowing lines of energy, which weave together all of creation, coming up from the earth, like these reeds here." Don Juan swirled his hands clockwise in front of my face. "See the golden tubes of light, fibers that come out of the energy of the earth. See with the eye between the eyebrows." Don Juan penetrated me with a burning hypnotic gaze.

I have the sensation of an explosion in my brain and a single eye within my forehead becomes unsheathed. It is like looking through a perforation in a gelatinous membrane. Within the space of the perforation I can see into a world of energy. I can also see inside matter itself.

Don Juan continues, "Now draw upon one of those energy lines as if you were smoking it, breathing it in. Pull a golden-white mist to you and let it sink like a stone into your womb. See a glowing egg forming there."

I follow his mysterious instructions and am aware of a throbbing in my abdomen that pushes in and out like a bellows. I sense my inner energy begin to glow and expand within me, as I lose sensory awareness of the external and focus on inner light.

"From the egg there comes a vapor that sinks even lower until it oozes from under you and wafts around you and up your spinal column. It flexes like a mist of flame. When it hits your heart breathe in, draw it in again. Begin to see your lungs glow and your heart pulsing, burning. Soon there is so much of this energy in you that it has no place to go but up. A swelling oval of light appears at the center of your chest. Breathe in. The light is rising, growing, expanding. You're exhaling the glow. The oval opens. Inside is white-hot fire. The nose and mid-brow open as if you had snorted a sacred powder. The eyes begin to glow. The glowing vapor reaches the skull, which clarifies and hums like crystal. The vapor swirls inside the crystal. See the mistlike inclusions. The entire skull starts to exude glowing vapor. It smokes.

"Exhale and make a soft 'ha' sound. Drop the jaw, leaving the mouth to gape open. See a gray cloud of poisonous fire-gas leaking from the mouth, reducing everything in existence to ash. Everything but you and me. Emerge as the energy within the ash. Rise out of it. In the gray dimness of the gas you glow brighter and brighter with fire. Take it! It is yours! Take the empowerment!"

I actually feel a beam of light coming into my head and rooting me to the spot. It travels through me like a huge channel. Don Juan exhales before me. I see his eyes glow with green fire. He rivets his eyes on me and raises his right arm like a snake. The palm of his hand turns down with the back facing me. I see an eye open on the back of his hand, like an eye in the center of the forehead. He extends two fingers like fangs of a snake ready to strike. He raises his left arm as if to call energy and then sends voltage through his two fingers directly into the muscles above my breasts. It feels like being bitten. The energy rushes into me, propelled by its pressure. I shudder and lose my breath.

My whole perceptual scope is expanding, resonating. Everything in existence is vibrating faster. A glowing golden doorway has opened before me.

"Before the white man came to our land, this river flooded every spring. Then in the summer, crops could be planted, and in the fall, harvested. Now there is a dam upriver. But back then, the only safe place to cross the waters was right here. Anywhere else, the current was too swift and too deep. This was our land. The crossing is still here. I will show you how to cross over into the higher realm of

energy right from this spot. It is mine to show because I possess the power of this place.

"Most people do not know what to do at the moment of death. In order to fight it, or to use its power, one must release the best in oneself. I want you to release yourself and cross the river of energy. The glowing egg you perceive is life force energy. It's your best beginning. Each time it opens it will move you. Golden-white ovals will shower you with life, healing, magic. Because you release this energy it will return to you magnified. This is the great art of manifestation and creation. Furthermore, each time your energy will travel farther, farther into the great sea of all life. I now give you this crossing.

"Listen well. If the moment of your death arrives you'll leave your body like a giant golden-white egg burning with a Dream Body inside it. There'll be a shimmering sheet of light before you and a river of energy beneath you. You'll walk on the water and begin to vibrate more rapidly. It'll appear that you're dissolving through a barrier. Cross the river of energy, then exhale and explode like fire through the barrier and you'll find me on the other side waiting for you. This is the power I give to you. I am the only person who can bestow it. With this power you'll see into other realms and you may even attain the great art of crossing with your body while still alive.

"You have a destiny. What brought you here years before and what has happened now happened by design. Otherwise you wouldn't be with an old Indian wizard like me. In return for what I'm going

to show you remember that at some time you'll have to share this with others.

"You'll begin to see vortexes in your waking world. You're forming a bridge between energy and matter. You may be able to transmute almost any illness and make incredible things manifest. These are gifts you should share. If you practice Smoking Skull no knowledge will be denied to you, providing your heart is pure. Once you've become powerful enough you'll be able to call down, raise, and transmit energy the way I've done for you. I reveal these things to you because they're going to happen and you need to prepare for it."

"What did you do to me in the fire pit? It was like a ritual cremation."

"Exactly. You were dead. After that I penetrated the very core of your being with energy. I give you these gifts because I've cared for you. They're mine to give and they're now your legacy. They're like no other. You've been taken by power itself. Now stand up."

I'm trembling. Don Juan is terrifying me. "After you witness this final act, you'll have to leave this place. You'll sleep for a while, for many years, then awaken and remember that you have a task to perform. After its completion, I'll call you and you'll leave the world with me." He stares at me fixedly until I am totally still. Don Juan is holding my arms. He begins to transform himself.

I sense a self-willed silence in me. I cannot pull out of it! Don Juan bores into me, fixing all of my attention. When he has my whole focus, don Juan explodes into light, burns like a supernova *before my eyes! Rays of golden white-hot fire shoot out of him and penetrate my very being. The lenses of my eyes close down in the blazing light. I'm grappling with blindness! Every atom, every cell, is burning to the core. Oh, my God! What have I done? What have I seen?*

Part 2

Healing the Dream

CHAPTER

eight

❀

Twelve years passed before my deeper memories began to resurface, coming in the form of dreams. Until their arrival, I was truly asleep. My feelings had become deadened. I lived life in an empty material dream. I even wondered if my few memories of don Juan and Chon were not merely hallucinations. I suspected that, in my awful grief following Richard's death, I had simply gone mad. To hide that suspicion from myself and others, I pursued graduate school and a teaching career in an escapist academic trance. Then my awakening began with a dream late one night.

I find myself in the foggy highlands of Chiapas, Mexico, sitting in a hovel filled with the smoke of the incense copal. Outside Mayan hunters trudge through the snow carrying a sick jaguar on a litter; the animal is in pitiful condition and is treated carefully. The hunters stop outside my doorway. The jaguar removes an eyeless white stone mask from its face and throws it on the snow. The hunters move on. I consider my situation, cowering close to the door. I decide to retrieve the mask.

Just then a Mayan warrior priest, dressed in a cape of jaguar fur, walks up to my door. He digs his feet into the ground and raises his arms to heaven in a hieroglyphic dance, and he appears very threatening. The priest throws another mask, which is as spotted as a jaguar pelt, onto the snow. It lands closer than the other. I know that he wants the white jaguar's mask and is prepared to fight me for it. I decide to acquiesce. When he looks away I take his mask. He picks up the white mask from the snow and walks into the mist.

I was awakened from this dream by the phone ringing. In the dark I rolled over and groped for the receiver. I was disoriented and had no idea of the time. The caller was my general practitioner, Dr. Melville Stickle.

"Merilyn, I got your message. Are you still feeling bad?" he asked in his deep country drawl.

"Yes, doctor, just terrible."

"And you're taking your medication?"

"Yes, of course." Turning onto my back, I held the receiver in one hand and touched my forehead with the other. I was still running a fever. "I can't seem to shake this thing. I can't eat. I cough until I vomit. And my fever is so high, I can't shake the chills."

"Merilyn, there's someone I think you should see, a

specialist at Sacred Heart Hospital, Dr. William Babbitt. I want him to do a complete workup on you."

"Okay, Dr. Stickle, if you think so."

"Good. I'll set up the appointment for tomorrow morning."

"Tomorrow? But it's Saturday."

"He sees patients on Saturday until noon. Get there as early as you can."

I was now very concerned. What was the matter with me? I had already missed a week of work and assumed that my students were vegetating. I had not felt well since taking them to witness the landing of the Columbus ships. I could not sleep at night. One of the things that preyed on my mind was how my classroom had burned down recently. My students and I were painting a mural of the Mayan pyramid to the god Kukulkán on the large back wall of the classroom. We had just completed the drawing when we left school that Friday evening. Over the weekend the entire language wing of the school burned down. It appeared that the fire had started mysteriously; its cause could not be determined. The whole incident bothered me terribly. I felt that somehow there was a connection between the fire and the onset of my illness.

The next morning I awoke to the sun peeping through my window. Even after a night's rest I still felt physically weaker. I got dressed and left for my doctor's appointment, wearing my wool coat and running my car heater on full-blast on this warm, sixty-degree day. I coughed and hacked all the way there. Finally, I reached the hospital and searched for the entrance to the underground parking for the cancer center. I found it and pulled into the first open parking space. Getting out I noticed a nice black Jaguar sedan nestled in the spot next to my Jeep.

The glass doors of The Cancer Treatment Center braced and slapped open as I stepped on the rubber sensor floor mat. Inside was a reception area with a kindly overweight receptionist in a purple pantsuit with a poodle decal. She was slurping cinnamon drops and looked at me curiously.

"Do you have an appointment?"

"Yes, with Dr. Babbitt," I stammered, leaning slightly against her large wooden desk and helping myself to a candy.

"What's the name?" She was turning the large pages in her roster.

"Merilyn Tunneshende," I said, but the woman just stared back, looking confused. "What's the matter?"

"You're not on the list."

"Dr. Stickle made a personal arrangement with Dr. Babbitt to see me this morning. I'm not a regular patient of his."

Partially convinced, she called "downstairs" to check. "You can go down," she said, hanging up the receiver. "He'll see you. Take the elevator to the basement and turn right."

I rode an elevator down one floor and shuddered when the door opened onto a scene straight from hell! Cancer patients. Some people were tottering with walkers and appeared grayish-yellow and agonized. There were old people and young people waiting around, some sitting and others leaning against the nice furnishings for support, orchestrated to the soul-numbing music in the background.

In the center of this grand alien temple, like an altar, stood the records hub. The white-smocked clerks, busy behind their pink Formica counters, generated the files of the chosen. I tottered up to their sanctuary.

"Merilyn Tunneshende?" I asked, not even sure myself.

From behind the counter a woman folded her arms and just stared at me.

"For Dr. Babbitt," I stuttered. She signaled to another woman who said, "Come this way," and then led me through flapping lab doors into the chemotherapy treatment section.

I was stunned by the dark energy I perceived, evidently due to the effects on the patients of chemo- and radiation therapy. Patients lounged around in recliners with IV bags attached to nearby poles, like moored balloons. Unlike those waiting in the general lobby, these patients had a greenish-gray tone. I watched a medium-sized blond man in a lab coat scooting around between the IV bags, as if he were checking the helium levels of the balloons to be sure they did not deflate.

Could this be Dr. Babbitt? I was escorted into an examination room and left alone with the door closed. I sat as still as a bunny hiding in the grass until the door opened and this man stepped inside.

"Merilyn, I'm Dr. Babbitt." It took all my strength to get up from the chair. As I struggled to stand, I caught a glimpse of myself in the wall mirror. I was horrified! My clothes were hanging off me. My face looked like a skull covered with gray mummified skin, and my sandy hair hung like oily straw down to my spiny elbows.

Dr. Babbitt saw the reaction to my mirror image and gently pushed me back into the seat. "Sit down, Merilyn," he said kindly. His eyes were already spinning in alarm. I could imagine his synapses were firing in rapid sequence.

I now got a good look at him. At first glance you might have thought that he was Scandinavian. A very Nordic look, commanding. Hair all sunlight with a shock of moonlight at the forehead, mildly waved. Under the fluorescent light a whitish glow emanated from him. He had delicate but masculine hands.

"Let's talk about your symptoms," he suggested. "Fevers?"

"Yes, about 103." I watched him write this down.

"Night sweats?"

"Yes! How did you know?"

He shrugged off the question. "You're coughing. How long have you had that?"

"It started around Thanksgiving, but it's gotten worse since Christmas. And this is what, February?" I hacked.

"Yes. Any weight loss?"

"About twenty pounds over the past month," I said, looking down at my now emaciated body.

"Swollen glands?" He looked at my neck and throat.

"Not that I'm aware of."

"Nausea?" His list seemed endless.

"Oh, yes."

"I need to examine you, Merilyn. If you can just step over to the table." He walked out into the hall and called a nurse. When she came into the room, Dr. Babbitt proceeded to knead my neck like a piece of bread dough. His fingers then flew lightly up and down the sides. "You didn't feel these swollen glands in your neck?" He seemed alarmed.

"No. I don't usually feel there."

He stared at me with grave concern. "Have you been out of the country?"

"Yes, often. Most recently in Mexico. I was working on a grant for the NEH. Do you think I got something there? I've never gotten sick before, except for the occasional gastrointestinal bug."

"I'm not sure. What do you think you have?"

"Dr. Stickle thought it might be mono, but I'm not improving with rest."

"If this is mono, it's the worst case I've ever seen," he

snapped, then added more gently, "I'm going to check you into the hospital. We'll run some tests."

"All right. You do what you think is best."

He smiled. Doctors are suckers for compliance. "So what was this grant you were working on?"

"I was researching the roots of Hispanic muralism as an art form in the pre-Columbian murals of the ancient Maya. My NEH grant allowed me to spend three months in the jungles and the mountains of the Yucatán Peninsula. I did a lot of linguistic work toward my doctorate as well."

"Are you fluent in Spanish?" He seemed intrigued.

"Yes. But I'm not Hispanic." I started coughing again.

"Excuse me, Merilyn," he said graciously. He now stepped over to the counter and clicked on the intercom, whispering orders like an obscene phone caller into the speaker, assured that his staff would respond instantly.

I was retrieved by a wheelchair attendant and hastily admitted *a la carrera,* or in transit, flying through the tunneled bowels of this radioactive underground site to the elevator and emerging on the eighth floor of the hospital. I was then shuttled to room 800 with barely enough time to reel in my tongue from soaring around the last corner.

My room was small and private—all the rooms were private, I was told—with a huge plate glass window. The view was of a modern high-rise topped with a neon pyramid. Night was falling, and I could now finally rest. The pyramid glowed insistently in the dimming light. At some point while observing it, I drifted off to sleep.

There was a full moon over the neon pyramid at my 4:00 A.M. temp check. Mist was rising out of the exhaust vent outside and spiraling up past my window. My sheets were damp. My pillow was soaked from fever-induced perspiration.

I hear clay flutes and ankle cymbals. The top of the pyramid is bathed in a blinding white light. I am teleported, kneeling in a hewn limestone chamber before a stone altar. I am overtaken by this genuine waking vision. Groping blindly in the light as if swimming through some unknown substance, my lips pronounce indecipherable soundless words.

The light begins to condense more brightly on the side of the altar opposite me. It solidifies with unbearable tension until it shoots upward like a giant translucent tombstone, out of the floor. At its sides are sharp, angular, whitish-yellow winglike emanations. In the center of the luminescent tube is a brilliant vertical crack, a place where two worlds of light collide. It is from this crack that the being of light speaks.

"What are you?" I ask, my hands clasped in front of my heart.

A sound booms in response. I feel the braille of hieroglyphs, swimming symbols of light, being transmitted from the light source to my fingertips on the stone altar. My fingers fly like those of a blind woman across abstract, luminous thoughts. The hieroglyphs turn into small snakes of light biting my tender fingertips with sharp fangs. I continue to feel them writhing under my touch.

"I am here to bring you back to the one who remembers you."
The light seems to envelop the chamber. It condenses again in front
of me.

"Who is the one who remembers me?"

I see a hand of white light emerge from the central crack of the
radiant being. I feel it tenderly, gently, caress my cheek. Light glows
from it like steam from dry ice. The hand is cool and soothing.

"Remember," a voice is saying. I have a flash of total clarity. I
know what is happening to me. I know what is going to come.

C H A P T E R
nine

~

I lay in my hospital bed several nights later. The day had passed in a daze with nurses traipsing in and out of the room, taking blood samples or trying to entice me with cups of orange sherbet made of frozen guar gum and orange #3. I waved them off with disdain. I barely looked at the food they brought; the smell was quite enough.

The moonlight burnt through my window, glistening like little pearlescent ponies rushing down a mountain, kicking up dust. I gazed at the moon, which covered me in a spotlight. I raised my arms into the flow of light. They were bathed. I sensed that it was time for me to go again, into the moonlight and into the silence.

I begin to lift out of my body, drifting and floating upward. I feet myself rising freely and then I find myself again traveling through another realm.

The mists of Dreaming thin to reveal the land of the Mexicas, ancestors of the Maya, in central Mexico. This is an aerial view of the pyramid to the sun at Teotihuacán. The pyramid planes down, celestial, massive, almost like a natural mesa but stepped. I know that underneath this pyramid are caverns from which the antecedents to the Mexicas crawled at the end of a great flood, spurred on by faint rays of sunlight spraying through the crevices. Above the caverns they molded a mound, built upon time and again until it became the largest "New World" pyramid, second only to Giza. I know that before the flood it was colder here and that men hunted mastodon, and earlier there were many belching volcanoes amid the dense vegetation. I recognize it all at a glance. I sense that it is about A.D. 0. The Native American groups are mostly wandering. Corn has been domesticated and water is of primary importance.

Time slips ahead and it is now about A.D. 300. The descendants of the wandering people have settled in the southern Yucatán peninsula, where it is very tropical in some places but almost arid in others. Legend has it that off the coast of this land a giant asteroid crashed from the sky, kicking up dust, blocking out the light of the sun, and plunging the world into cold grayness. The people develop astronomy to watch for and predict these phenomena. They carry on traditions of mound-building, arts, and agriculture. The men are very strong and hunt the wild creatures.

The scene moves forward in time to the edge of a natural formation. It is a huge, circular, freshwater pool, almost bottomless, surrounded by porous white limestone and trees. The peninsula is honeycombed with these sites, and they are sacred. The seawater seeps through the limestone, which naturally filters out the salt, making the water fresher. At the bottom of these pools lives the rain god Chac. He shows by the level of the water if he is pleased or displeased.

A water priest, one who can interpret Chac most effectively, stands at the rim of the formation. The wind is blowing. The horizon is darkening. The priest is dressed in a linen cloth worn below the waist like a skirt. He is shouting to the sky.

"Just as the great spirit of the waters, Chac, brings water for new life to our lands and takes the waters back," the priest shouts, "so the life his waters bring he also takes. In this way, I, the servant of Chac, offer him this newborn life in the hope that he will allow our crops to be born anew."

It is the dry temperate season, when Chac must be appeased. If he brings back the waters they will come with the great heat. There are shouts from the crowd.

"Chac, we are thirsty! Chac, bring us water!"

A baby is grinning those funny little colic smiles. His parents stand dutifully close to the edge, about one-quarter of the way around the pool.

"He is going to throw the baby into the water!" someone shouts.

I consciously enter this Dream. "Don't throw in that baby! His new life will be swallowed up!"

Someone shouts and points from the crowd. "Let us see what he will do with her!" Another man points to me. "We can offer the baby later if we need to. This is a new way. She is offering herself."

"This is a new way," someone else yells.

"A new way!" the crowd chants.

The parents walk around the path with their baby. They are to wait in a ceremonial hut until morning.

"We'll throw you in at dark," the priest snarls, glaring at me. His eyes glint as he stomps off to his hut to bask his thoughts in the smoke of copal, leaving me to stand at the edge. The people ring the pool at a distance and peer at me for a while. Then they disperse, muttering among themselves. I sit down and hang my legs over the edge. It is a long way from the bottom of my feet to the water. I wonder if it will be cold or warm.

While I am sitting there thinking, I hear a rustling in the jungle. Out of the foliage comes Chon, bronze and taut, with teeth as white as the moon. He still wears cropped hair with bangs and a white tunic. He carries a small bundle of tied-up green leaves in his left hand. I am overjoyed to see him.

"This is the entry you've Dreamed. We've been waiting for you to wake up," he says, examining me curiously. "We're going on from here. Chac is old and fathomless. He'll not spit you out. He'll transform you. Chac is spirit. Let me share this with you." He points to his bundle and rubs my limbs with it.

Chon then rubs my entire body with an aromatic mixture of animal and vegetable greases. While he applies the ointments, day becomes night. The priest returns and Chon vanishes into the jungle.

"I'll not even throw you in. Get in yourself," he snaps.

"But there's no way down," I say, looking into the dark water.

"You'll have to jump." He looms over me. Behind him the wind is rustling the trees.

I consider using the vines to lower myself and then hanging onto them throughout the night, but the priest watches to make sure I jump. I have no choice. He now pulls out a flint knife and comes closer. If I do not jump, he will kill me. There is no one else present. I hear him growl. I jump. My stomach gives and my legs fly up, smarting as they hit the ice-cold water. I cannot breathe. Then I feel myself drifting.

"Don't control. Release yourself to Chac's energy," calls Chon's voice, as he walks out of the jungle.

I open my eyes. It is pitch dark, but I feel that I am floating on the surface of the water. I draw a breath. Phaa! But I can move my head around to get pure air.

"Jaguar grease," Chon says as he steps over to the pool's edge, "and aromatic plants to keep the heat up. You just stay as you are. The moon will be up soon. She'll also have to decide. That priest is threatened by your power. He said, 'If she floats and is dead, it means Chac has rejected her. If there's no trace of her body, it means Chac has accepted her.' He walked off as soon as you jumped."

I remain in the water. Chon speaks of how time and Dreaming are circular. They always come back. Then the moon rises. It is completely rounded. When it arcs to the top of the sky, the moon is directly over my pool of water, and I am suspended in a giant glowing white ball. I move just a little to make ripples in the luminescence.

"I knew it," Chon cries triumphantly. "Stay within the moon. You'll be a seer. Just remain as you are and listen to the birds until dawn." He disappears into the forest again.

I try very hard to listen just to the birds, but every now and then there are animal cries, terrifying noises that bubble out of the darkness. Eerie cries that make me think of some older soul. Finally I see a hint of purple and scarlet in the sky. I then hear a crowd coming down the path. Chon is hopping around like a blackbird, shaking a vine he has gotten to pull me out.

"Chac has blessed her," he shouts at the crowd. "She's neither dead nor rejected. She's alive in there."

A vine slaps down into the water. "Stop talking nonsense," the priest says as I grab onto the vine and they pull me out. "Chac has not even acknowledged her attempt."

"He has!" Chon insists.

I am dripping wet and covered with green grease and sludge. My cloth garment is also translucent green and hangs clumped, barely covering one thigh.

"This is an abomination," the priest hisses, plunging his flint knife into my side.

There is darkness and a sense of rising. I am again floating over this same site in the jungle, but now there are many more people here. The place is teeming with life. Multiple stone constructions and pyramids abound. I see a spiral structure, an astronomical observatory.

I float down like smoke and assemble, seated cross-legged, in a dark corner of a training site set aside for females. Here they are instructed and live out their lives until they are "called for." Chon is seated with me. I admire his kind, careworn Mayan face with its long slender nose. He smiles and points to the billowing mass of clouds above the observatory.

"I've been waiting for you. The offering to Chac has changed. If we're going to advance this knowledge any further, we have to heal its sacrificial aspect."

"What year is it?" I ask myself. I see from the hieroglyphs to the Lord, on a stone stela—like a totem outside the Nunnery—that he reigns in the year equivalent to A.D. 650.

I hear the heavy steps of the Halach Uinic approaching, jade clinking. He eclipses the sun as he blocks the doorway, peering inside. He is huge, tall, strong, and powerful. I look in astonishment at Chon.

"Welcome to Chichén Itzá," growls the Lord. His teeth are studded with precious jade and turquoise. He leers at me and then moves on, followed by two lesser nobles dressed in robes of jaguar fur.

I am now taken on a tour by Chon. There are man-made cisterns in the ground and underground water flowing over hot embers for steam baths. On the coast, toward Tulum, are sites for ritual bathing and purification so divine they seem celestial. We *are swimming underground in clear water, bathed by sunlight from round holes cut into the cavern roofs. Dolphins are leaping and wriggling within and without the water-filled caverns leading to the sparkling sea.*

We travel by dugout tree-trunk canoe up a river through the jungle to another site, Palenque, rather far from Chichén Itzá. The lord there, Aháu Pacal Votán, has even installed an underground sewer system, and he is constructing a huge Temple of Inscriptions to house his remains. Like the Halach, he is a tremendously large man, but he is pale and clubfooted and has eyes that turn out.

Inside his palace's Chamber of Initiations people perforate their tongues and genitals in an ecstatic bloodletting ritual to obtain visions and to divine with the spattered blood. A species of mushrooms is eaten or powdered and smoked to produce hallucinations that are intensely revelatory. The visions and divinations guide the participants, out-of-body, through the realm of the deities.

As we trek through the jungle back to Chichén, our jungle path narrows and then disappears as we begin to rise, spinning upward like vapor above the lush foliage. When we next descend, time has moved forward. I see a courtyard of tremendous stone cylindrical objects suspended on ropes, which workers in loincloths push to sway. When struck, the cylinders make a deep chiming sound that carries for miles. There are non-Maya faces mingled in the passing group. The Maya practice head-flattening and -heightening, and most have beaklike noses, which are absent in these people whose noses are smaller and sharper and who have rounder faces. They are fierce-looking and their costumes are different, more warlike.

I read on a stone inscription that it is now A.D. 1200. I am made aware that these alien people are descendants of the Toltecs, who were chased down from the north. They have settled in Chichén and revitalized it. Chon and I walk past the huge step-pyramid on our right, dedicated to the prophet Kukulkán, or as they say in their language, Quetzalcóatl. It is aligned with the sun, and the light forms little triangles on a long series of stairs, descending and rising like a serpent's body into the stone heads of gaping snakes. Kukulkán is a powerful deity of transformation.

We proceed slowly along the courtyard, which leads to a tall, wide, rectangular temple with stairs. At the bottom are stone columns extending almost endlessly around the temple; more than 1,000 surround it, holding up its long, thatch-covered passageways. This is their Temple to the Warriors. A multitude is gathered in front of the immense temple. I move to the end of one of the thatch-covered colonnades.

Chon emerges with me from the crowd, his face showing his concern. "We have arrived. This is what we've come to transform. Sacrifice has become something from the underworld." I nod in complete agreement.

The Maya are chanting. The Toltecs are holding back an agitated crowd. I begin to push my way through the mass of agonized people, who are screaming in languages foreign to me. I have to See.

The Toltecs stand aside and let me pass until I arrive at the base of the steps. Then one of them grabs my arm to escort me up the steps.

"I don't need your help," I say and pull my arm free. I mount the stairs, which are extremely steep and covered with terracotta and multicolored hieroglyphs. The climb is very long. There is a hush in the crowd as the chimes sound. When I reach the top, I behold a reclining red stone god with a huge belly plate at the head of the stairs. At the four corners of the temple, overlooking the jungle, there are kneeling stone figurines holding cups in which to catch the "nectar from the gods." The massive head of a snake sits behind and to the left of the red stone god.

The incense smoke creates a fog around me. Suddenly I experience vertigo from the height. Through the smoke I detect the pyramid to Kukulkán in the distance. Out of a stone chamber emerge two Toltec priests dressed in red woven robes with golden eagle's head helmets from which their faces peer. They each take one of my arms. And then out from behind a stone partition struts the Halach Uinic, resplendent in green quetzal feathers, like an emerald aura, a spectacle unto himself.

He glares at me with satisfaction and begins to scrape an obsidian blade on one of the ceremonial stones. Chon huffs and puffs his way up the steps to us. He brings a ceremonial urn of medicinal fat. Chon regards me with great empathy as he rubs the fat over my chest and whispers a prayer. My chest is heavy, and it is very hard for me to draw a breath. My skin is also tingling, floating outside itself.

Chon stands aside and the two Toltec priests escort me to a stone slab. Holding my arms from either side they bend me backward over the slab, while two lesser helmetless priests tie my feet together to the ring of stone on the floor beneath. The Halach Uinic bends down over me.

I whisper, "I am not afraid of you." From behind me one of the eagle-helmeted priests holds both my arms over my head; the other steps to the front and pushes me further backward against the slab, bending me deeply at the waist. The Halach leans over me. I can feel his heavy breath on me. He surveys me.

"I'm not afraid of you," I repeat glaring back at him. "There is nothing more you can do to me."

"This is where you take your power!" Chon calls out from the side. "After this, you've tasted the worst!"

I stare into the eyes of the Halach Uinic and see his fear. He is afraid he will lose a battle. His eyes are feverish and his temples begin to perspire. With his knife he bears down hard on my sternum, splitting my chest open. He sticks his hand inside my body and pulls out a bloody treasure: my severed, still-beating heart. The Halach gasps as he glares at it. My heart begins to glow golden fire. Below, the crowd sways in slow motion. The Halach throws my burning heart onto the belly plate of the red stone Mool.

ten

D r. Babbitt stopped by early the next morning with a chubby young medical student at his side. The boy had pudgy fingers protruding from his ill-fitting lab coat sleeves and a baby pink-white face. Bracing myself against the sink and looking into the mirror, I was braiding my hair under a fluorescent bulb.

"Merilyn," Dr. Babbitt began haltingly, "we've found out something."

"What?" I turned around to look at him.

He took a deep preparatory breath. "You've got . . . AIDS," he finally blurted out, glancing away from my startled look.

Silence. AIDS? Oh, my God! I did a double take in disbelief, but it was as if Dr. Babbitt was moving in slow motion, peering at me out of the corners of his eyes and making it hard to read his expression. I turned and looked glassily out of the foggy window.

My energy was breathing outside my body, slightly behind and above it, attached to it by a silver cord through my abdomen. I hovered there in total shock. The medical student turned his face toward me. It was becoming flushed and looked hot and damp. I reached for the railing on the bed and pulled myself back onto it.

"AIDS?" I struggled to whisper.

"We don't know if it's full-blown yet."

"The blood work came back?"

"Yes."

"It's impossible. You SAW the virus?"

"We detected the antibody that fights the virus," he said sullenly, still staring out the window.

"Do the tests again!" I cried out.

"I will," he said, looking fully at me for the first time, his voice anxious.

"There's been some mistake!" I shuddered.

Dr. Babbitt watched me hold the railing, then glanced at his flush-faced neophyte and left the room with him.

The next day I began to devour the current medical literature on AIDS, circa 1992, from the nursing library. Each article I read was more discouraging and pessimistic than the previous one. A lovely nurse named Fauna solemnly brought me these encyclopedic, weighty, dusty volumes at my command, as if she were retrieving them from the library at Alexandria.

"Merilyn, do you really think you should be reading all of this?"

"I've got to know, Fauna."

At some point I began reciting the names of these biological demons to myself over and over, sweating as I turned the huge pages of the Necronomicron.

The doctors came in to perform a TB skin test. I was informed that if my immunity was low I might not have a skin reaction but could still have raging tuberculosis. The health care workers were wearing facial masks.

Later, at about 10:00 P.M., I awoke to hear a discussion outside my closed door. An angular beam of light flooded the darkness, and two people made their grand entrance into the ante area. The nurse, Patsy, wearing a face mask, was accompanied by a small, well-dressed, delicate man with graying hair worn long in the front and behind the ears.

"Merilyn, I've brought someone to see you," said Patsy from behind the mask.

"I'm Doctor—"

"Rosco Bostik," I interjected, sitting up in bed to extend my hand to him.

"How do you know my name?" he asked with a thick accent, offering me his small, cool, well-manicured hand.

"You've heard of me?" He seemed baffled.

"Dr. Babbitt told me you might be in to see me this evening."

"Oh, well, yes," he said. "Did Dr. Babbitt also tell you that I'm the foremost authority in the state on HIV/AIDS?"

I nodded my head. Dr. Bostik seemed pleased with his notoriety, and he pulled a chair over to my bed and elegantly sat down, crossing one leg in the dark. "If you'll excuse us, Patsy, we're going to talk for a while."

"Of course, Doctor." Patsy walked out of the room, closing the door behind her.

Dr. Bostik observed me for a moment, triangulating his hands in front of his face. He took a little blue paper mask out of his jacket pocket and placed it on the table beside him. "I'm not going to wear this thing. I can't stand them. And, besides, I'm immune to tuberculosis. I had it as a boy." He paused for a moment, leaning toward me slightly. "Merilyn, tell me about yourself."

I was encouraged that he had survived tuberculosis himself; given his current age it must have been in the thirties, before antibiotics. And despite his immunity I was also touched by his gesture.

I haltingly began, "I'm a thirty-nine-year-old school teacher."

"Yes, I know that," he said patiently. "I've talked with Dr. Stickle. I mean, tell me about your illness."

Somewhat taken aback, I peered at him through the shadows. I began to enumerate my symptoms of fevers, night sweats, weight loss, weakness, cough, and fatigue. Bostik listened attentively, almost with fascination.

"What have you been told, Merilyn?" he asked sweetly.

"That I have AIDS." I watched his reaction closely.

"And how do you feel about that?"

"Well, I suppose they want me to believe them now. I mean, they've shown me the blood workup," I whispered, scooting down the bed to get closer to him.

"What a philosophical outlook!" he exclaimed. "And how were you told you had AIDS?"

"Dr. Babbitt just walked in here and said 'You have AIDS.'" Dr. Bostik winced and looked away, adjusting himself in his chair.

"What else have you been told?" he asked after he had recovered.

"That I might also have TB, even though my skin test was negative."

"Yes, that's possible," Dr. Bostik said somberly. "Merilyn, the thing for you to remember is that although we don't have a cure for AIDS we can treat most of the symptoms. Now I need to examine your eyes." He opened his black doctor's bag and pulled out an ophthalmoscope. "Come down to the foot of the bed," he said, patting the bedding. "When I turn this on I want you to look into the light."

He held the instrument to my right eye, and I stared into the light as instructed. He tried to examine my eye. "Don't look at me, look into the light." But I wanted to look at him. He had soft wrinkles on his forehead from years of caring service, like the rumples in an old baby blanket. My mouth opened a little as I stared wide-eyed at him.

"Merilyn, don't look at me. Look into the light," he insisted calmly.

Look into the light. That phrase recalled vague memories of another experience. Staring at the lighted ophthalmoscope, I saw just the dazzling white brilliance at first, but then *I detect a tunnel with an even greater light at the end. I can feel the molecules of matter being sucked out of me and down the tunnel, chasing one after the other in an electric dance, a freeing spiral. As they funnel into the tunnel I begin to hear warbled notes, like birds tweeting, that turn into voices calling me from the tunnel, from underneath the archway of an old stone bridge. One is a beautiful female voice.*

"Merilyn," she says.

"Nanu!"

It is my great-grandmother. She is standing under the bridge in a long, high-necked Victorian dress of midnight blue. She looks beautiful. Her long, thick auburn hair explodes in a halo around her high cheekbones and creamy forehead, and then winds to the back of her head in a bun. Her huge almond eyes glisten their perfect ice blue. She is holding up a burning torch that reveals the workmanship in the stones above her.

"Merilyn?" This voice is deep and liquid.

A slender, well-dressed man with equally hypnotic eyes emerges from the shadows of the bridge and stands beside Nanu in the light. I recognize him instantly. "Richard!" I gasp. I feel my heart break-ing, pounding, my eyes tearing. My breath races as I rush toward them, getting closer and closer to the spark-filled torchlight. They move backward into the shadows under the bridge shaking their heads "No." I hear Richard's voice say, "Stay." Dr. Bostik turned off his ophthalmoscope.

"Are my eyes all right?" I asked, disoriented and anxious, wiping my tears.

"Yes." He looked quizzically at me as he placed the in-strument in his bag.

"Do you think I have AIDS, Dr. Rosco?"

"What we know is that you're definitely HIV positive, which is . . . unfortunate. I haven't gotten the CD4 report yet, which will show the condition of your immune system. When I get that I can tell you more. I feel, however, that you've had this a long time." He pondered for a moment. "Once you're infected with HIV the count of T4 helper cells goes down about one hundred cells per year. The normal count is around one thousand. I feel that in your case you might want to look back as far as twelve or thirteen years."

I am shocked. "You think I've had it that long?"

"It's quite possible. Both HIV and tuberculosis can lie dormant in the body for years."

"Well, there was a rape," I stammered.

"And before that?"

"Just my fiancé, who died."

"Died?"

"Yes, in an automobile accident."

Dr. Bostik looked at me knowingly. "I think you might want to consider that . . . casual contact as a possibility." He nodded his head and sat back in his chair. "So, you're a linguist, I'm told? Can you guess what country I'm from?"

"I'm just a Spanish teacher, Dr. Bostik."

"But I bet you speak it perfectly."

"No one speaks any language perfectly."

"Only a linguist would say that."

"Very well, I'm a linguist then," I conceded. "I should be careful, though. I don't want to insult you." I peered into the bluish-gold light that now surrounded him and let its female texture whisper to me. It softly conveyed *Don't say Yugoslavia. You'll startle him.* I blinked my eyes. "I'd say that you're from Romania or Bulgaria," I pronounced.

Dr. Bostik looked completely flabbergasted. "I was born two hundred and fifty miles from the Romanian border, and one hundred miles from Bulgaria. I'm a Yugoslav, a Serb."

Dr. Bostik adjusted the red respiratory isolation sign on the door, pulling it closed as he walked out. I thought, lying back in my hospital bed, that I was used to isolation. I felt tugged strongly by it, as if my physical matrix were dissolving, as if my illness were enabling forces to pull me more deeply into them.

I Dream that I am trapped in the cement cell after the rape. Heavy footsteps are approaching and I am terrified. The wooden door swings open.

It is the Halach Uinic standing in this dumping alleyway. He is dressed in his linen tunic, with woven grass thong sandals, and with a small woven straw-and-quetzal-feather headdress adorning his head and long black braid.

The Halach squats in the doorway and sits down on the edge of the filthy mattress, looking around at the trash with some unfamiliarity. He lights the oil lamp and sets it on the floor, and then takes an obsidian blade and a small clay container from his pelt bag. He uses the blade to slice the flesh of his forearm. The Halach extracts a powder from the container and pushes it into the wound.

The light from the lantern sputters. "Ah. There you are," the Halach says, seeing me hiding in the shadows, or perhaps his senses have been hallucinogenically heightened.

"So, you have not managed to get away from me. What do you have to say about that?" he asks flippantly, pressing a small piece of crude paper against his bleeding arm.

"I don't understand what you want with me," I say, coming forward into the circle of light cast by the flame.

He burns the paper in the fire of the lamp. "It is not so simple. Since the beginning, you have opposed me. I do not know what you expected when you offered yourself to Chac. You seem to believe there is some uplifting transformational force at work here. I, on the other hand, know that the only way to survive is to perpetuate what exists throughout the changing masks of time."

I am stunned by his eloquence. It reminds me of the saying that the Devil has a silver tongue.

"You will not easily recover from the memory and experience of all that is happening to you now," he says with certainty. "The energy that you expend in these futile attempts at transformation will be mine. You will also be harnessed into maintaining the order of the world as it is."

"Why do you want all of this?" I gasp in horror. "Why would you go to such degrading lengths? Surely you realize that choosing this way will be your undoing. The world cannot go on as it is."

"All of this," he replies, with a sweeping gesture of his hands, "is the only premise we can be certain exists for the moment, and it must go on." And with that declaration he rises from his seat and leaves, locking the door behind him.

After sitting there trembling and weeping in the dark for what seems an interminable time, I hear a noise at the door and brace myself.

I growl and then roar like a jaguar, "I won't live like this! You either kill me now or let me out!" I start to beat on the cell walls. Then a blinding flash of light fills the dank cell as the door cracks open. Standing in the doorway is a man of medium height and build, wearing a lightweight white tunic and robe. He has brown wavy *hair and his whole body is surrounded by celestial golden highlights. There is a small party of Mayan flute players with him, and several Maya cast flower petals around his feet.*

He opens the door of my cell completely. It creaks on its hinges. "You have unlocked the secret," he says. He then turns and leaves with his following.

"Come with us," one of the flute players cues to me in Maya.

"Who is that?" I ask, scrambling to my feet and trying to follow this enigmatic man and his procession.

"That is Kukulkán!" one of the flower-throwers excitedly informs me as the party passes through the barred gate to the street, leaving it hanging open.

eleven

~

I awoke from Dreaming as Dr. Babbitt walked through the door. "Merilyn," he exclaimed, "I've got great news. Your TB is not contagious anymore! That means we can let you go home!"

Immediately my friend and fellow Spanish teacher, Liz, and her husband, Guillermo, came to my aid. At my request, they and their children cleaned my two-story house from top to bottom, and I had Liz put it up for sale. She then went grocery shopping for me and prepared and froze my first week of meals, while her husband serviced my car. Other teachers brought more food by the house, while some of my students dropped off flowers, which Liz set out in lovely arrangements.

I was overwhelmed. Everyone was so nice. When the day came for me to check out, Dr. Babbitt stopped in early to say goodbye and set my next appointment; I wore a pretty dress Liz had picked out for me. While I talked with my doctor, she carted my stuff out to the car, and then came back for me. Liz sat me in a wheelchair, topped off with my ice pitcher, and then hauled me out of there. We arrived at my home a few minutes later.

Climbing the stairs to my second-floor bedroom was a grueling experience. Holding onto the hand railing, I slowly pulled myself up step by step. Liz had cleaned the room, which was sunny and smelled of fresh flowers. She then left, saying she would be back at dinnertime to heat up one of my frozen meals.

Looking around my room from the cozy double bed my eyes lingered on all the Mayan lore I had collected. Small pre-Columbian figurines smiled at me from the window seat. A picture of Chon—the only photograph he ever allowed me— hung to the right of the dressing mirror.

At the foot of my bed was an old oak hope chest filled with handwoven blankets that I had brought back from various trips. It also contained notes and stories from my talks with Chon on Mayan Dreaming and other subjects. Although Liz had told me to get up only for the bathroom I felt compelled to retrieve my notes. I was now particularly interested in his talks on Kukulkán.

With some difficulty I opened the heavy lid. The chest smelled of wood and wool on the inside. At the bottom, under all the folded blankets, I found several large notebooks filled with the *Dreamings of Chon*. I hopped back into bed as fast as I could, expecting Liz to barge in and catch me at any moment. Thumbing through the voluminous pages, I was reminded of the great amount of notes I had taken. My eyes were mesmerized as they lit upon the relevant topics.

Mayan Dreaming: A Journal of Chon's Revelations

~ The Chicxulub Asteroid

"The original mother place of forming intelligent life consciousness in this system was Venus. This is why the Maya revere the second planet from the sun. However, during her formation she was struck by an asteroid. This impact released so many noxious gases that the surface heated to a degree that prevented the evolution of organic life. The focus was then shifted to Earth, but on the third planet, life was already developing according to another matrix. The consciousness of what we know as humans had to wait.

"About sixty-five million years ago, according to the scientists who are always investigating around here, the Earth was also struck by a large asteroid we call the Chicxulub. It hit off the coast of the Yucatán, not far from this place, and its arrival made the way for human consciousness. All the huge reptiles that then inhabited the face of the Earth died out in the cold caused by the dust that blocked the light of the Sun. So to the Maya, the Chicxulub is sacred because she bore great blessing and also great transformation.

"It was still a long time before Man could emerge. The changes in the temperature of the Earth Mother caused many surviving creatures to grow fur and carry their young on the inside. Finally, from these existing beings something like humans evolved, but the planet was still very cold in many places. The cold would intrude and then recede in cycles. This caused the need for migrations.

"The migrating protohumans would stay underground when the ice was too great. They hunted large animals that could feed them for a season, as the meat remained fresh due to the cold. Major migrations began about two hundred thousand years ago, according to our calculations. After a long, cold, and windy era, the dust kicked up by Chicxulub began to clear, and the Earth Mother started to warm up. There was later a great flood caused by the melting of much of the ice.

"During the time of the flood, water vessels were built. Some were small but others were great in comparison. The peoples migrated until they found land standing above water and there they settled. This ended approximately fifteen thousand years ago. Even with the height of some of these lands, it was once again necessary to seek refuge deep inside the Earth, as the waters continued to approach.

"Finally the waters receded, and the peoples began to emerge and occupy the lands where they now found themselves. Approximately ten thousand years ago, with most of the ice melted, the lands were freshly inhabited by the ancestors of the people you find there now, although some boat migrations still continued. We, the Maya, settled here in this warm tropical womb, and as our culture grew we began our astronomy to measure these cycles of transformation, such as issued in the Chicxulub."

～ The Tzolkín Calendar

"As I have told you before, the Maya have a sacred calendar called the Tzolkín. It begins in 3313 B.C.E., during a cycle of collective revelation, and ends in A.D. 2012. Actually though, to anyone who understands the calendar, it runs backward from the later date to the initial. The reason for this is that the Maya calculated that Man would slowly lose the picture of divine evolutionary manifestation, which is the beginning matrix of everything, due to the fact that he began here improperly.

"In the year 2012, among many celestial signs, the planet Venus, home of our original matrix, will pass across the face of the sun in a tiny eclipse. Life here will undergo another transformation, such as the one that was brought

by the Chicxulub, sixty-five million years ago. At this time
the possibility of our higher vibrational matrix will again
manifest.

"During the last Katún, or twenty-year cycle, from 1992
until 2012, the Earth Mother will gradually withdraw her
life force energy from the planet to facilitate this transition.
Many species will become extinct. Human beings will
experience disturbances in their sexual energies and powers
to reproduce. The lands will not be able to support everyone and many will go hungry, which will cause aggressions,
cleansing the burden of too much unsustainable life.

"It is at this time that people will begin to remember.
They will remember the Chicxulub, and how we got here,
and the divine evolutionary matrix. Each man at this time
will act according to his purpose. Some will entrench
themselves, hoping to survive and make off with what is
left over by others, only to find themselves dead at the
beginning. There will be those who seek to ease the suffering of life and thereby earn great energetic merit across the
Spirit Waters. Then there will be some whose awareness
will leave the Earth Mother in her entirety. They will go off
in search of new worlds."

I paused from my reading to reflect. I noticed the sun descending on the horizon, and I could see the colors changing to golden roses from my second-story bedroom window.

I picked up my notes and continued reading.

～ Kukulkán

"The name *Kukulkán* means 'feathered serpent.' This is often misinterpreted by those who do not understand native culture to signify some type of flying dragon. What the symbolism actually means to those who created it is the combination of the most high being with tremendous sexual energy. A particular line of evolution happened when the consciousness evolving for Venus shifted to this place of reptiles.

"In this part of the world, we experienced manifestations of this energy taking the shape of the Uay Kin, or Sun Being, and also of the Eagle Deity. A total manifestation was called Kukulkán, as is only fitting. The energy showed itself in these lands as they now exist well before A.D. 50, encouraging people in peaceful agricultural and highly artistic practices. However, it was eventually forced from its site above the great Teotihuacán by rivaling and emerging energies. When the manifestation departed it foretold of its return. And so the prophecies began.

"Another full manifestation came to the people around A.D. 700, to the world of the Toltecs and then to the southern lands of the Maya. Kukulkán came as a noble and a prophet, preaching an end to human sacrifice. A rivaling warrior priesthood conspired, frightening the people with

stories of what would happen if the sacrificial bloodlet-
tings—to appease the god's transformational appetites—
were to cease. Chased out of Tolán, the capitol of the
Toltecs, and then chased from Chichén Itzá where he tried
to reestablish himself, Kukulkán maintained that life must
evolve, as do the deities.

"The ruling nobles tried to kill Kukulkán. He left,
promising to return in the year One Reed, which, as history
showed, is the exact year that Cortés arrived here with his
first boats of Spaniards. I have heard stories that in other
cultures Kukulkán appeared at different times, but of
course I cannot vouch for those."

As I closed the pages it occurred to me that the contents
were more than just extraordinary. These Dreams were elegant, rare, and very encompassing. Chon was an artist of
Dreaming.

As the sky darkened I heard Liz put her key in the lock. I
quickly hid my notes under the comforter as she trudged
up the stairs to say hello. By the time she got to my door I
looked completely innocent.

The next day we went grocery shopping for goodies that
Liz had not anticipated. I used one of the motored carts
with a small front basket to accompany her down the aisles.
Although I was extremely embarrassed to have to use this
cart, I could not resist the urge to toot the horn and come

right up on her heels. Naturally, I did not tell Liz of the haunting images as we debated choices of cheese doodles. At last she deposited me at home. I could return to my notebooks with a full belly.

~ The Final Age Before the Sixth Sun

"If you look at what has happened in our long history, you will see then what will come. The first good wave was brought on by First Man and Woman [Black Africans]. They stimulated each of the peoples, enhancing their genetics, migratory urges, and reproductive powers. The less-developed men, thus stimulated, then wreaked havoc in successive overflowings, but these periods would sometimes stabilize and evolve. Finally the last wave of all came: the White Man, which ended it. When the Earth Mother recalls the life force, she will again start with First Man and Woman, who will once more send ripples throughout the species. There may be famines and sickness in Africa. There may be saints on that continent. Perhaps by then White Man will be at the peak of his scientific and spiritual development for this age and may have something positive to contribute, in order to smooth things out, but this is optimistic.

"During this last epoch other major shifts will occur. All the peoples' wisdom will pour out and be shared in an effort to build a bridge through what is to come. Meanwhile, species will vanish from the face of this domain. Scientists will look to the heavens in an attempt to predict and defend against another Chicxulub; simultaneously, humans and other creatures will be dying of every conceivable thing here on the Earth.

"Since female wisdom is the only manifestation that stands a good chance of prevailing after the shift, there will be a transition toward the feminine side of things in the hopes of aligning life with that which sustains life. Women will emerge with enlightenment in all cultures. These events will reach a high frequency in the last Katún, or twenty-year cycle of the Tzolkín calendar. After that time a truly spiritual consciousness will be born and unto it a world that will be the highest vibratory manifestation in this system until the Seventh Sun, when all things will again rejoin with the Creative Dream."

The telephone rang. Somebody, a female professional, was ready to make an offer on my house. After talking with her I turned on the educational channel and saw a short piece about the possible application of Star Wars technology to deflect incoming asteroids, as well as a special on the Chicxulub asteroid's possible connection to the extinction of the dinosaurs. That was the last synchronistic straw. I simply could not disregard the signs any longer. Something important was happening, and my energy was intimately involved. If that was the case then it was required at the highest decision-making level. I had a contribution to make to how this would turn out. I decided to follow my destiny, to override the traditional medical advice and return to Mexico during the month it would take for the bank to put this woman's loan through. I needed to find Chon and deal with my illness at a higher level and to release myself to this rapidly unfolding process.

I was not sure I could ever find him. I would start looking at Palenque, but that was a very remote area of Mexico and twelve years had passed. The last time I had seen Chon he was crossing over into another realm. Maybe he never returned. But I sensed that if I was going to claim my power this was the starting point. And I knew that it would once again be a life-and-death struggle. At just that moment, on the Spanish television channel, the musical background accompaniment for a commercial was "Canción Mixteca," one of Chon's favorite songs!

twelve

ᔕ

Like a Dream, the Aero Maya charter to Palenque was fueled and waiting when I flew into Mexico City. After a brief passage through customs, in which a kind Mexican gentleman helped carry my bag, I walked out to the small twin-propeller plane with the pilot. He appeared to be in his thirties and of Mayan and Mexican heritage. He asked if I had been ill. I told him that I was recovering from tuberculosis.

The flight was relatively short. When we reached the mountain range that dipped down into the jungle, the pilot flew below the clouds so we could admire the view. The rippling green blanket extended to the sunlight as tropical fronds opened, bidding us welcome. We descended onto a minute landing strip. I accompanied the pilot to the charter office.

152 ~ Healing the Dream

My head was swimming. The jungle periphery spun and undulated. It was as though I were walking through the open center of a whirlpool or a forming spiral galaxy. My midbrow throbbed and my ears buzzed. I called a cab from town to retrieve me and take me to Esmeralda's restaurant.

In about twenty minutes the cab drove into the parking area at the front of Antojitos Mayas. When I stepped into the restaurant and looked around I did not recognize the young Mayan women working there. I went up and asked one of them if Esmeralda was about, still extremely unsure of myself.

"She's in Guatemala," the young woman said, peering at me like a bird.

I felt a lump in my throat. She was gone. I would never find Chon. My energy settled into a gentle acceptance of impending death.

"The only one watching the place is her brother, the old curer," she added. "Do you want me to call him for you?"

"Yes," I gulped.

The young woman went off to the huts in back of the building. Within a few minutes I heard Chon's singsongy voice and melodious laughter approaching.

"Ah! My prodigal Merilyn . . ."

I now saw him! He stopped several feet away with a huge grin on his face, cocking his head at me. He did not look very different! Same big smile. His hair had not even grayed much, which was not unusual since many Maya maintain their blue-black hair into their nineties.

"You return! Happy day! Happy day! Welcome!" Chon stood back and regarded me with a keen eye. He patted me on the back and gave me a big hug around the shoulders.

I went limp and dumb. In shock, I could not think of a thing to say. I dropped my bag to the ground and just stared at him. I was so happy to see him that I almost died from joy, as my life rapidly passed before my eyes.

He laughed. "Well, I guess you're staying for a long visit." He cocked his head to the other side, observing the huge suitcase at my feet. "Come back to the hut and rest. We can talk about it all later." Smiling, Chon led me through the tree-shaded common area.

I could not believe my eyes as we walked to the curing hut. Was it possible, I thought, that I was really here with him again? I looked around and noticed that there were no patients lined up as usual. That seemed odd, surreal. Chon watched me, as if I were waking up from a dream. "I felt there was something coming up," he said gently.

As he motioned me through the opening into the smaller thatch hut I sensed another presence inside. I strained my eyes until they began to adjust to the poignant darkness. Finally I was able to make out a body swinging in a hammock off to the side, in the back, behind swirling smoke.

"Well, well, well . . ." a male voice called out, as the man rolled out of the hammock. I could see that he was tall, and the voice sounded very familiar. He walked through the copal smoke toward me. As faint rays of light hit him I beheld a recognizable figure. For a moment I could not possibly believe my eyes, waiting for my vision to clear. But it only became sharper. I was totally taken aback! Standing there in coppery brown slacks and a shirt was don Juan. I fainted.

Nine days passed in a blur. Chon kept me semiconscious with some kind of plant potion and incantations. Whenever I awoke, he would feed me more and I would slip back under. I have vague memories of him, or don Juan or both of them, standing over me and chanting. I also recall once ordering don Juan to explain what he was doing there and hearing their cackling response.

When I was finally allowed to rouse I had a tremendous appetite, and they kept bringing me trays piled with dried fruits, roasted corn on the cob, avocados, mangoes, and bananas. It was as if they were trying to solidify me. I noticed there was some kind of salve on my chest and I could smell the aromatic plants in the hut. Copal smoke hung in the air. My breathing was now much clearer and my formerly low-grade fever had broken. I felt a profound, ethereal state of well-being.

One afternoon Chon brought in a plate of figs. I sat up in the hammock eating them and began recounting the whole story of what happened after my crossover in Catemaco—about my rape and flight from the underworld. I concluded the account with my recent dreams and then the travail of my illness and hospitalization. Chon squinted at me.

"Ah. Hmmm," he said cryptically. Don Juan stooped under the doortop and came inside, walking over and lying in the other hammock. His hair was much whiter but otherwise he looked the same. He was holding Chon's new friend, a large blue macaw, perched on his index finger. He got comfortable and took his time before talking, as always. I was moved by his beautiful countenance again as he gazed at me from the shadows. The macaw squawked in agreement and flapped its wings, flying in slow motion to one of the rafters, where he peered down at us.

"I can't figure this out," I mumbled to myself.

"It's going to take a lot of figuring," Chon cackled. "I think the first thing we'll have to do is take you to the sacred place where my special plants live, and present you to the energy that watches over it. We should offer some of your blood to the ground there in the hopes that the energy will share a Dream of how we may transform it. Then we will visit the temples and ingest the mushrooms. I told you one day this would be necessary. Your self-sacrificial blood must be in the broth, and we will put the sacred powder into a fresh slice in your flesh."

I grimaced. Chon took out his divination board and

emptied his pouch of seeds and crystals onto it. He began counting. He went on grouping seeds with a sleight of hand reminiscent of shell-game sharks.

"Southwestern native peoples also have prophecies concerning these times," don Juan began. "The Earth will wobble like a top on its axis and the magnetic poles will shift. This happens in cycles. It's transformation. Whether we're in harmony with the planet or not is of great importance during these times, as is the purpose of every being when the whole of creation begins to spin with the force of this shift." Don Juan's hands made an elegant and forceful conjuring motion.

Chon smiled with understanding and looked up from his divination board. "You are being asked to open a gateway," he pronounced solemnly.

For the remainder of the afternoon don Juan entertained us with his flute playing and I became acquainted with Manik, Chon's new little baby monkey. In the early evening, I fell asleep, but periodically awakened to hear Chon and don Juan talking into the night. The whole setting had a dreamlike quality, almost as if this were really an outpost at the edge of infinity.

The next morning we rose early and ate tortillas and homemade cheese before trekking into the jungle to visit Chon's sacred place. Fortunately it was not very far, nor was the day too hot. Chon said it was very important that I enter walking. We arrived at a small grove down a winding foot-path, a distance away from the top of the waterfall. There myriad plants were growing, and I was sure Chon had precisely transplanted them to this place himself.

At the back edge of this grove was the upper portion of an ancient carved stone head sticking out of the ground. "Go sit in the center there," Chon directed me as he unpacked a copal urn and lit some wood chips for embers. He placed the smoking urn and flower petals in front of the partial stone face. The smoke began to curl upwards. Slowly it appeared to assume the form of an ethereal woman of mist. "Look at her," said Chon.

The woman changed into a hag. "Don't be afraid of her. She has many faces," Chon whispered to me, sitting close and watching the smoke for answers. Her foggy eye sockets became hollow and her face turned into a floating skull. She then extended the bony curl of a smokelike limb to me. Its fingers wafted open. "Give her what she is asking for," Chon insisted, his eyelids half-closed.

I pulled out a small obsidian blade from my pocket and sliced the flesh between my middle and ring finger as Chon and don Juan had instructed. I held my fingers open with the hand down so that the blood dripped onto the earth beside me. The smoke figure transformed into a horrific shape that reminded me of *The Scream*. Finally she settled into the ground, and we dug a small hole on that site where

we dripped more blood and covered it with dirt. After giving thanks in the form of thoughts, gestures, and burning
copal lumps, don Juan and I left the grove. We walked back
together in silence, while Chon stayed behind for a long time
to "talk to the spot."

That night I swung in my hammock in the dark listening to the howler monkeys, whose calls did not bother me,
and to the birds, whose night repertoire was diverse and most
beautiful. Little Manik played with my finger and jumped
around on my stomach as I fed him peanuts in the shell.
Finally he wrapped his tail around my neck, and we both
fell asleep.

It was several days before Chon renewed his talk about returning to the temples and performing the mushroom ceremony. In the interim don Juan and I walked great lengths
and feasted at the kitchen hut. We made frequent trips to
the waterfall to "listen to her singing," and to cool off and
watch the butterflies.

"Did you ever learn the trick I told you about long ago?"
don Juan asked one sunny day, as we sat on the bank of the
stream with our feet in the cold rushing water.

"Which trick was that, don Juan?" I asked, considering
the breadth of his instruction.

"Dreaming you're an animal," he replied with a tolerant
smile on his old tan, sharply chiseled face.

"Oh, that old trick," I said nonchalantly.

"You'd be surprised. You see, your jaguar spirit is sick. You have to find another to fight along with it. Try to get a different animal helper to come to you."

"How do I do that?"

"Open yourself up and be silent. Think your intent into the out-there," he explained, lifting his hands with a sweeping gesture. "Then lie down on this smooth rock and go to sleep for a while. I'll be back later to check on you." Don Juan stood up and walked downstream, leaving me there on the bank by myself.

I yawned. A butterfly tried to fly into my open mouth. I blew out a little puff of air to shoo it away. Sitting quietly, I wondered what kind of animal would come to me. The nearby falls sounded like a woman giggling. Slowly, in this peaceful natural setting, I became very sleepy and I placed my face against the smooth stone.

My rising awareness is engaged by the tiny presence of a lizard doing push-ups on the rock directly in front of my face. It seems to be demonstrating how it exercises. We stare into one another's eyes for a moment, both a little embarrassed. It continues its push-ups before finally scooting off. The same butterfly now lands on the slightly upturned tip of my nose, making it itch. I rub a finger across my upper lip. The butterfly floats away again.

I hear don Juan calling me to alertness; I know that I am Dreaming. In front of my face, there is a small explosion of light and a shaking sound. A huge rattler is now sitting coiled in that glowing place, sunning itself on a boulder opposite me and across the waters.

"What do you want to know?" it asks me, raising itself up. Then it partially lowers its head and flips its tongue out.

"How can you help me?" I think to it, my head heavy with deep Dreaming.

It slithers into new coils, hisses, and rattles, then raises itself up again. "If you must make friends with the venom, you will shed many skins." The butterfly lands on top of the snake's head now. "Transformation is within this symbol." The rattler's yellow eyes roll up to look at the butterfly, forming a small golden triangle. A halo appears around it. "Remember this sign," the butterfly-crowned serpent utters. "This is your energy. It will belong to you and the ones you walk with. As for the Earth and beyond, I do not know of any creature who will not guide you if it is able." A large golden hawk lands in a tree behind the reptile, and the vision flashes out of existence.

I awakened to see don Juan sitting cross-legged on that same boulder.

As I told don Juan of my Dreaming, he acknowledged that talking to the rattler was a very auspicious sign, since snakes possess blood and transformational wisdom. He said the butterfly was a symbol of transformation and of resurrection. The crowning of the serpent with the butterfly spurred profound reflection in him. "Which of the creatures that appeared could you Dream of as yourself?" he asked solemnly, giving the impression that my choice was of grave importance.

"All of them, but I feel most like the golden hawk. I have often had flying and soaring dreams," I said, splashing cool water on my face.

"I'm often a bird myself," don Juan said, smiling with approval. "When your energy soars it can be very healing. You'll have great vision. Don't land too close to the ground; land on high. But you must remember to land or you'll never come back. When you hunt, just as it was with the big cat, be skillful, merciful, and quick." He stepped across the stream on a row of stones and handed me a hawk feather.

thirteen

"Merilyn," Chon said somberly to me the following day while he cleaned plants at the table in the kitchen hut, "there's something we need to talk about. You must understand that you did not fully sleep when you came to Earth. That's why you have the dreams you do. Most people act out their purpose with unconscious motivations, never really understanding what they do. I'm afraid that's not the case for you, and once you begin to shake off the sleep it never completely comes back."

"What are you trying to tell me, Chon?" I asked him with a feeling of dread, drawing my knees up to my chest as I sat on the bench listening intently.

"That the higher your spirit flies, the more you'll remember, like a hawk seeing a vast view of what is before her and of what lies behind. If we go to the temples and share the mushrooms your spirit will rise to a vista loftier than dreams, and you'll see much more than has already come to you. You must be prepared for this.

"I believe the disease you carry was released by the Earth Mother in the last Katún before the new era begins. Its origins can be cured. Don't be afraid to look at that part of it. If there's to be any knowledge gained or healing brought back, you must be willing to examine everything. I am sure that your courage in going deep and facing the truth is one reason you were selected to struggle with it.

"There is another matter, that of your transformation. You'll get glimpses of these things. They're extremely important because they give you an understanding of what is happening to the world as a transformational whole. You must go into the ceremony knowing all of what I have told you."

"Will you and don Juan participate with me?" I asked.

"Yes. Our paths are shared. We go with one another. If you have more questions formulate them during these final days before the full moon. Once she is full your thoughts must be complete."

"You think we will find a cure for this, Chon?"

"If we do, it'll come from the Earth and beyond, not just from men. This was what all our prayers and offerings at my sacred place were about." For some reason I felt better knowing that Chon and don Juan planned to ingest the mushrooms with me. I spent time anxiously thinking about the ceremony, trying to imagine what it would be like. Beyond this curiosity my mind was mostly blank. However, I did not have the luxury to vacantly drift very long in this state. Within four days the moon was full.

On the day of the ceremony, we all awoke early. It was still dark when Chon prepared herb teas in the kitchen hut. He would not allow us to eat any food that day. There was an eerie silence around the place. Even the wind seemed to be still.

Before dawn Chon left us and went to damp wooded areas about three miles from the ruins to collect the mushrooms. Don Juan and I sat in the hut and stared at each other.

"What's the real connection between us, don Juan?" I asked him across the table.

He looked at me from above his steaming mug. "Your energy is close to leaving this world and traveling beyond it. Mine has already left it. I came for you. There's an integrity that's shared between us. That's the way I see it. When I first spied you in Arizona you reminded me of the occasional spirit traveler who came into our lands before the coming of the whites. For three nights before your arrival I heard the howl of the train in my dreams. You were what I was waiting for. I felt you, even when you were a little girl.

That is why I was standing there at the train station. You know by now that I put my own energy into you." I gasped as I fully remembered the last time I saw don Juan. His eyes burnt.

"There's another connection between us and that's through the Feathered Serpent. This is a history shared by many native peoples throughout the Americas. It took different names but the teachings were the same. Some say it was coming with the final piece of prophecy to these lands that were unknown to the rest of the world. Others say it was a being who escaped death and changed its body into light.

"Nevertheless, these revelations to a visionary people should have been recognized and respected for what they were. At the coming of others to these lands, there could have been grounds for commonality and exchange. This, of course, did not occur. What the whites did was try to obliterate native knowledge, and they thereby threw away a piece of the answer to some of their most profound questions. They forced the Indian to accept a lesser reality, and in that way pushed the whole merging consciousness into their darkness.

"Native peoples held to their knowledge in secret, and now every piece of the puzzle fits together as they all come to move into something new. Formerly unrevealed knowledge is being shared. Prophecies are reaching outer limits.

What the new world will be is of great concern here. Matter is separating from spirit. Its vibration should be increased, spiritualized to form a unified, transfigured whole. This is what Kukulkán revealed."

Don Juan thought for a moment. "Its mark is on you. That's what I saw when I first laid eyes on you."

"What mark is that, don Juan?" I looked at him wide-eyed, cocking my head to the side in amazement.

"A light in the center of your forehead. Here. About an inch deep inside." Don Juan reached across the table, and with the first two fingers of his right hand he touched a place less than an inch above my eyebrows. I intuitively knew that he and Chon had the same light glowing. Don Juan gently smiled at me and retracted his hand.

In the late morning Chon returned from his trip to the woods. My chin fell to the ground when I saw the size of his sack; it was as large as a lawn bag. Don Juan burst into hysterical laughter and slapped his hand repeatedly on the wooden table. Chon smiled apologetically.

"Merilyn thought she was going to nibble one or two," don Juan managed to say between deep gasps for air.

"Why do you think you can't have any food?" Chon asked as he collapsed on the ground next to his sack, also overtaken with laughter. The expression on my face must have been pretty entertaining.

"Really, Chon, you can't expect me to eat all that!" I

shrieked, standing limp under the mango trees between a couple of rolling hyenas.

Chon wiped tears from his eyes with his weathered hands and patted the sides of his cheeks where he was smiling too broadly. His hair flopped over his ears. "Some will be boiled," he finally reassured me, shaking his head and still laughing to himself.

"All that?" I yelped. That started the two of them laughing again. I became disgusted and went off looking for Manik, hoping to play with him until these two composed themselves. When I came back with the monkey, don Juan and Chon were trying to be serious.

"Don't you want to see them before I put them in the pot?" Chon asked me, as if he were baking cookies.

I walked over and took a peek. The sacred mushrooms did not look anything like I had expected—like the large multicolored toadstools from *Alice in Wonderland* perhaps. These resembled the nipples from baby bottles, or maybe slimy little partially opened umbrellas. They were brownish-gray with a purplish spot at the tip of their cone tops. And there must have been fifteen hundred of them.

"Are those really them?" I finally asked. Chon put his hand over his mouth to contain himself, while don Juan stood up and walked away from the sacks to have a good laugh without disturbing me. Manik scrambled off my shoulder and onto Chon's. He hung his tail around Chon's neck and tried to swing down and snatch a mushroom. They seemed slicker and more delicate than any edible fungi I had ever seen, but then I was no expert. I sighed.

Don Juan came back carrying a huge, heavy black cauldron. He quickly built a fire in the center of the shaded area under the mango trees and filled the iron cooker about half-full with water from the rain barrel. When the water began to boil Chon started putting enormous amounts of mushrooms into the bubbling liquid. They cooked down fast, but he kept adding more. The pot soon contained a lumpy, molten brownish-black sludge.

During the afternoon I would walk by and stare down into the cauldron, afraid of what I would see. The substance was so shiny that it looked like hot tar. I could even see my troubled face reflected back at me. And the liquid became darker and thicker as it cooked down. Finally Chon transferred this molasses-like substance into a clay carrying pot and sealed it with a lid. There was about a half gallon of concentrated potion when he was finished brewing.

Chon went to his hut and brought out a small urn of powder; he told me that this was the same thick liquid spread thinly on a wax paper and allowed to evaporate. Don Juan was busy shredding dried mushroom specimens and wrapping up the stringy fibers like pipe tobacco in a buckskin swatch. I had never seen so many mushrooms in my life.

In the early evening we took bucket baths with rainwater. Chon dressed in a purple tunic shirt and drab green jeans. He added his jade beads and pierced earplugs. Don Juan wore a midnight blue cotton shirt and black denim pants with a bandanna as a headband around his forehead. His chin-length, thick white hair glistened. I was impressed by the decorative dress, as if naked were not good enough for the spirit world. I slipped into a rose-colored, washed silk tunic and slacks, and inserted the puma claw earring don Juan had given me years ago. We looked approvingly at one another and then headed up the path into the jungle, along the stream from the waterfall, and down toward the ruins.

It was late twilight when we arrived. Chon was carrying everything in woven shoulder bags. He signaled for us to walk past the Temple of the Inscriptions and head toward Pacal Votán's palace and the chamber of initiations within it. The structures shone brightly in the light of the full moon that was already rising. The place was completely silent. Not even night birds or cicadas were singing yet.

We entered the center chamber of the palace with the four columned, elevated platforms. Chon took his northern position and don Juan the one to the west. My spot was on the south platform, as it had been the first afternoon Chon brought me here. The night sky was a dark, lush tapestry above. It would be a clear night with many stars.

Chon walked down to the center courtyard between the

four platforms and lit the ceremonial fire. After it began burning well, he placed the clay carrying pot on the flames. Don Juan unrolled a pipe bag and extracted a long deer antler and bone pipe. He offered the pipe to the four directions and then to the fifth, the zenith. He then loaded the bowl.

"We'll proceed in rounds. First the smoke, then the brew, the fresh, and last the powder," Chon said, checking the pot over the flames. He climbed up to his position on the northern platform. "With each successive wave you'll be elevated higher. As more of the mixture gets into your bloodstream and hits your brain you'll catapult into another realm. These movements are often accompanied by flashes of light. You must maintain the intention of what you seek. You'll fly extremely high and very far, but it's imperative to remember to land, otherwise you won't come back and in the morning we'll find your dead body lying here on this spot."

I felt like a cold rock had sunk into the pit of my stomach. Don Juan lit the pipe bowl and took a long draw. He did not exhale the smoke. Don Juan smoked for a while and then stood up and brought the pipe to me. I puffed. The smoke tasted somewhat like dirt. In time I walked over and handed the pipe to Chon, who reloaded the bowl, smoked awhile and then brought it back to me. For every bowl they smoked I had to smoke two. At one point Chon went to the eastern platform and placed a six-inch hand-carved soapstone goddess upon it. He said she was Ixchel, the moon and water goddess. She would bring us back with the descent of the moon in the morning. He told me to listen for the sound of the babbling stream as I returned to my body. It would be a guide to pull me back in.

Slowly I begin to notice the whine of the cicadas getting sharper and louder. It feels like the sound is sawing or piercing my brain. Chon comes over and leads me to the center fire, where he opens the pot. With his obsidian blade he makes an incision between the second and ring finger of my right hand. It hurts, but somehow I do not feel like I am fully participating. The blood drips into the pot. My hand is wrapped and I go back to sit down on the south platform. I have some trouble deciding which platform is mine.

The pot comes around. Chon starts it. With each pass one must dip into it with a tiny clay ladle and slurp the contents. When it comes to me I notice the vessel has four emerging beings, one for each of the directions, decorating its sides below the clay handle. I cannot seem to focus on them. The potion tastes and feels like sod in my mouth. It is not at all sticky, as I had anticipated. The flavor is very bad, but not so bad that I cannot finish the spoonful. I believe Chon has put some honey and flower sweeteners into it. However, the problem is the aftertaste, which is very metallic and grows exponentially stronger with each taste, becoming overwhelmingly dominant. And the belching! Horrendous!

I feel that I will retch up the potion each time the pot comes around, but there is really no sensation of nausea, just the dread of the aftertaste. Actually, my body begins to feel very pleasant, quite euphoric. I am not sleepy in the slightest, as I had expected. On the contrary, I am exhilarated and hypersensitive.

I look about at the surroundings. Everything is so intensified I keep glancing from one thing to the next. The rustling trees seem to be whispering messages. I can hear and feel the tinkling of the water rushing through the underground system beneath us. Don Juan and Chon look somehow enhanced. It is as if they move in glowing slow motion.

Chon lifts his tunic and slices across the flesh above his heart with his obsidian blade. He opens the small urn and presses mushroom powder into the wound. Then he covers the site with fig bark paper and massages in a clockwise motion. Don Juan unbuttons his shirt. He takes his own blade and slices down the center of his chest at the heart. He also presses the powder in and massages the wound with fig bark paper.

Chon comes over to me with a third obsidian blade. I slice between my breasts. The flesh there is not as sensitive as I would have thought. I take a large quantity of powder and press it into the wound and then apply pressure with the bark paper, which stops most of the bleeding. I massage the area, following their example and covering it with fig bark. To my amazement, the powder disappears into the wound.

Chon walks back to his seat. The fire seems to grow in intensity and casts weird golden light across everything. Its crackling becomes all-absorbing, like background radiation. Chon and don Juan watch the fire with rapt attention. The top portion of their skulls appears to swell as the lower part narrows. The result has an almost lightbulb shape. I see a pink glow coming from them and shake my head in disbelief. Ghostlike vapor wafts from the tops of their heads. Sound stretches and distorts with every movement.

I do not feel the stone as being solid beneath me any longer, and yet I feel the pull of gravity. Rushes, like chills, start to move up and down my body in waves. I also feel the moon's pull and look up at the white orb. The light becomes silver. It is sticky and radiating. I am being lifted up like steam into its flowing beam. I perceive its glowing lines of energy and head along them toward the satellite. Closer and closer. Higher and farther. I release any desire to push myself back down into my body. I am almost free. My breath comes heavy and fast with excitement.

I begin to see the surface of the moon's craters, and then I hear an inner whisper inquiring where I would like to travel. My first thought is toward the sun. I now feel myself change direction and hurtle into black space toward a light in the distance that rapidly grows larger and soon becomes unbearably hot. I am going to collide and burn up. There is a blinding flash as I seem to accelerate in all directions at almost light speed. The force of this motion is so intense that I lose awareness of all other sensations but that of the movement and the light.

fourteen

I am beyond Dreaming. The mushrooms have propelled me into genuine shapeshifting. I move with everything—I am into simultaneous time and creation. After an explosion of light, I perceive a clearing and am walking through a shimmering golden oval toward the Ganges River, balancing a tall clay water pot on my head with my right hand. There is no detachment. I am fully present in this scene.

My dress is a large piece of orange silk wrapped around my body and draped over the left shoulder. My feet are bare. As I walk, I look to the left and see a spinning yellow-white light about the size of a dinner plate heading toward me. I quicken my step, knowing intuitively that the light is my exploding energy body and that, if it touches me, I will die in this scene.

The light chases me as it increases its gyrations. I run. It almost catches up with me as I reach an underground cooling shed on the banks of the Ganges. I step inside and quickly close the door behind me, thinking I am safe. I can see many water vessels in the light that sprays through a few cracks in the wooden door. As I take a deep breath of relief the spinning disk emerges out of nowhere and appears over my left shoulder again. It has been there all along! The light disk spins closer and touches the flesh of my shoulder blade and I explode into light.

At first there is nothing, and then comes the sensation of ash slowly settling into a cone-shaped pile. After a period that seems like three days, there is a stirring in the ash, similar to a breeze or a breath, and that becomes awareness. My emerging awareness easily passes through the wood and earth that make up the shed. I rise until I float freely above the Ganges. Spreading my senses through the air like wings, I watch men and women bathe and gather water. I listen to the music of their voices as I drift higher and higher above the river. And then in another explosion of light I blink out of this scene.

At almost the same moment I am a phoenix rising from an Egyptian tomb, a giant eaglelike creature of golden fire. As I burst forth from the ground, the oxygen feeds the force of my flames and my immense wings beat like bellows with the breath of magnetic energy displacements. Below people walk along the sands in delicate white linen garments. I watch the light around them grow stronger until there is another brilliant flash.

Bright awareness gives way and I perceive a light-filled dome-shaped chamber. The beings there are so golden-luminous that I can *hardly discern them; I mostly sense their presence. Their thoughts sound like voices, surging and rippling in my mind. They communicate telepathically, telling me to return when I have completely transfigured the body. They are alien angels traveling from another world. I am shown an abstract artifact of golden light etched with symbols. From its top a fountain of multicolored energy sprays, spilling upward like the genesis beam. It is the power of celestial crescendo, and its knowledge is encoded into me. Ecstatic, I explode into another flash of light.*

Light propels me forward and precedes my awareness, which arrives at a green jungle. I am amazed at my location. A group is gathered at the outskirts of a modest village in southern India, listening to Prince Siddhartha Gautama Buddha. It appears to be around 500 B.C.E., which means I have moved ahead a great span of time.

Prince Gautama stops his discourse to smile beatifically at me. He notices me assessing my situation rather than paying attention to the talk. I look furtively at the people around me and then turn my attention back to myself. I now realize that I am an ugly little man! I stare at my arms and hands in disbelief, examining them as if they belonged to those of a foreign species. This shapeshift comes as a tremendous shock to me but I am so enthralled by the Buddha that I turn back and listen to his words.

"You will struggle for a purpose in another land, Little Monkey Face," he tells me when I look up into his face. He is a spectacular creation with his big, robust body dressed in honey-colored silk, al-

mond moon eyes, and his flawless soulful features formed in the highest caste of India! "Purify life," he counsels me. "The best work is transmuting the low forms until they become the high. Seek to enter the clear light void."

I am enraptured by his words as Gautama points to the forest. I do not wish to leave the peace and humility instilled by his teachings, but he indicates that there is work for me to do elsewhere. He and his pilgrims traipse off through the lush, flowering Indian vegetation to the next small village. I sit in the woods alone. Soon it starts to drizzle. The patter can be heard on the green leaves. Off in the near distance, a tusked elephant cries out with an eerie clicking call.

I realize that I am not this little man! I am energy! This awareness causes me constitutional chaos. All the scenery's colors bleed like a watercolor in the rain. I am shifting into a rainbow bubble. Chon's words filter through as a guiding beacon, "Land or you'll never come back."

The resulting brilliant flash turns into the sun shining through jungle foliage. It is warm and steamy. I look at my body. It is darkly tanned and female. "This feels right," I say to myself in Maya. Looking around, I find that I am on a litter, being transported over a path through dense jungle toward a palace designated for the female ritual offerings. Male sacrifices must always be victims of war or ritual sport.

I languish on the litter in a cool white tunic while a small Mayan man holds a long bamboo pole topped with a round palm-frond fan over me to provide shade. I know I am here to finally and fully transcend and heal.

"Where are you taking me?" I lean over and calmly ask one of the Maya walking beside me in the procession.

"The Halach Uinic has requested that you be brought before Kukulkán," he tells me, his high black ponytail and white loincloth bobbing with every step.

"Am I not the chosen of the Halach?" I challenge him.

"Yes, Long Reeds, but yesterday the prophet Kukulkán arrived from his teaching tour of Uxmal. The Halach begged him to stay and bless our city with his knowledge. The Halach Uinic offered Kukulkán anything within his power to bestow in return for him remaining here in Chichén Itzá, making it the most powerful city-state in the world of the Maya." The man is completely carried away by his own gossip.

"And what did Kukulkán request?"

"He requires a sacrifice," the man informs me, as if that is always the natural pleasure of the gods.

"He ordered that a sacrifice be performed in his honor?" I pry, pondering my new fate.

"No, he desires that the Halach Uinic turn over his highest sacrificial honor to him for instruction," the pedestrian Maya corrects me.

Instruction in what? I wonder as we approach Chichén Itzá. We arrive at the Nunnery where I will live alone, visited daily by the Chuch Kaháu, who shall initiate me into the mysteries of cyclical time from his expert knowledge of the sacred Tzolkín calendar. He is waiting for me inside the hewn-stone structure and is lighting a wall torch when I enter. I walk over and douse my face from a basin of cool water. The Chuch Kaháu is Chon, fully present!

"Welcome! Welcome! Happy day!" he says, turning around to smile at me. Chon is wearing a white tunic that hangs to the knee. "Have you heard, Long Reeds? Have you heard the news about Kukulkán?"

"I heard it on the way back from the sacred well at the Bolonchén cave," I reply, recalling the vortex of spirit waters, my point of emergence.

"What do you think of his being here?" he asks. "It is a good sign." Chon smiles.

As we speak a large group arrives from a tour of the astronomical observatory across the way. Flute players and flower throwers accompany the procession. The Halach Uinic wears his finest quetzal feather headdress that sways five feet above the heads of the people. I hear him discussing recent advances at Chichén Itzá with someone in the crowd. At that moment the throng of people parts, and a man formerly unknown to me approaches the Nunnery.

He does not have the appearance of a god. His head is not heightened, and his skin is somewhat pale. He wears an ordinary white tunic, as do many of us, rather than fine ceremonial attire. However, there is a quality about him, a look in his eyes, and a special golden highlight around his waves of brown hair.

Now he does the unthinkable. He crosses the threshold of my dwelling place, which custom forbids to anyone other than my attendants, the Chuch Kaháu, the Halach Uinic, and me. I am at a loss for words. He gazes at me kindly in the light of the sun passing through the doorway. Chon steps back into the shadows.

"So you are the one who would die for transformation?" Kukulkán asks, surveying the sun's illumination of the carved relief stone walls.

"If you request it," I reply respectfully, trembling under my tunic.

"I could give you a choice," he says with an authority only a god could convey. "What are you called?"

"Long Reeds, Lord."

"And why do they call you that?"

"A long reed is strong because it yields to the force that moves it. It neither breaks nor is uprooted but bends, allowing that which passes to go its way. This is our concept of perfect sacrifice," I answer him.

He beams at me. "Does everyone think as you do?"

"Only I think as I do, my Lord."

Kukulkán nods in acknowledgment. "What I require of you now is that you answer my questions about Chichén Itzá. I will call for you each day. Do you agree to this?"

"I agree to your request, Lord Kukulkán." Kukulkán and the hordes of Maya then leave and continue their tour with the Halach Uinic. I sit down on a straw mat. Chon brings me some fruit as I

replait a section of my long black hair. He plops down on the mat beside me.

"You did well," he says.

"What did I do?" I ask, peeling an avocado.

"You were honest."

In the morning I am escorted to the field of ceremonial flowers by a young male Mayan emissary. He points to the center to indicate that Kukulkán can be found there. I walk through rows of fragrant tall lilies, carnations, and irises. In the midst of a magnificent section of marigolds I discover Kukulkán reclining on a straw mat, basking in the fresh light and fragrance.

"Good morning, Long Reeds," he calls to me. "Come sit beside me here," he says, patting the mat. I sit on my knees next to him. "What beauty, all the rippling flowers, no?" I agree with a nod of my head. "Tell me, how many gods are worshipped here at Chichén Itzá?" He is smiling.

"We have an entire Pantheon of gods. The principal deity of Chichén is the water spirit. We will, of course, incorporate you into our main worship, now that you are residing with us," I proclaim respectfully, using my training in political diplomacy.

Kukulkán seems unimpressed. "The Zápotecs to the northwest believe in only one energy, transforming but present in all," he says pensively.

"I am of like mind," I respond as the breeze blows.

"What do you know of me, Long Reeds?"

"*Your coming was foretold to us in prophecies that began with tribes to the north. You are a god of transformation, a teacher, a healer, and a bringer of peace.*"

"*I impart my energy,*" he replies. "*Do you know this symbol?*" Kukulkán draws two crossed lines in the earth between our mats.

"*That is the symbol of our male corn deity, Yum Cax,*" I respond with pleasure.

"*And what is my own symbol here?*" Kukulkán asks.

I draw a circle topped by a triangle in the dirt under his two crossed lines. "*Your symbol is the planet Venus. You see, here is the Earth, the circle . . . and here is the divine wisdom coming down into life in the form of a pyramid, this triangle.*" I smile with satisfaction at having correctly explained his hieroglyph.

Kukulkán smiles. "*Now look at the combination of all three.*" I gaze at the marks on the ground. The result is that the crossed lines sit upon the apex of the triangle, as our roof combs sit upon the tops of temples in my ancestral home of Nah Chan [Palenque]. "*This is prophecy. See this new sign. Have vision,*" Kukulkán commands.

I fix the symbol in my mind. It begins to explode with meaning, blossoming within my forehead. Kukulkán continues, "*This will have much power for change, good and bad, in the period of time to come. It must be passed through. It will purge, distill, and purify. Now tell me, how did you come to be at Chichén Itzá?*"

"*I was brought here. Seers are always from Nah Chan, just as the Chuch Kaháu all come from Tikal, where they study the calendars. When I was reported to have emerged, the Halach Uinic, who is from this place, was studying the wisdom of the Mayan dynasties at Uxmal, the university city. He ordered me transported here." I fiddle with a marigold stem.*

"How were you found?"

"The Priestesses and the Jaguar Priesthood navigate the energetic realms in a search for a female with visionary capacity and a complete womb."

Kukulkán ponders the situation with great reflection. "What is the purpose of your offering?" He is gazing solemnly into the endless waves of swaying flowers splashing with golden color.

"My own offering opens the way for transformation and transcendence. It is energetically evolutionary and hopefully healing. It also permits the Halach Uinic a glimpse into the mysteries of energy and spirit. My reward is my spiritual identity and my energy."

Kukulkán considers for a moment. "As enticing as that must be for the Halach Uinic, does he truly deserve such revelation without seeking it from his own heart, offering himself? In willingly offering the life of another, can he indeed enter into the higher realms he seeks? All your offering does for him is suggest the existence of awareness and energy beyond death. Unless he appreciates the value of the life being offered—the greatest altruism, the offering of one's own life—how can he travel higher paths?" He stares intently into my eyes.

I pause to reflect. I risk telling him my true feelings. "I believe that there is much to be learned from a sacrificial offering, but that in the final analysis one must transform oneself. One must do the work, not pull energy through others. Then there is also the value of sparing life and bringing it forth."

Kukulkán appears touched by my honesty. "The only sacrifice equal to the Greatest Energy and Spirit, the only one worthy of being practiced, is sacrifice of self. It is the only offering that will heal the world, evolve the spirit and provide the harmonious balance of energies needed to create life. It is the sacrifice that emerges as something higher. You shall merge with the fidelity and love that is waiting for you out there!"

Kukulkán stares at me curiously. "This knowledge is deeply pervasive at all levels. You cannot ascend without dealing with it. Every ascending energy must offer itself for something greater. What is offered is what matters most. Energy should be free: a flying, departing, and returning spiral being; blithe and abundant, an infinite explosion; an eternal, rippling feathered wave of dazzling color; the dance of love and sheer attuned force; and the boundless vibration of the spheres. Humanity does not See. It is like a stone-cold breast with no milk. Superficial. And Man is always exacting payment. Who gave him the right to charge for something he did not invent? You must know now what I prefigure. If you give yourself, you will have a choice. You will not be taken in some crude way. If your offering is for transformation, energy will empower it." Kukulkán stops for a moment to watch a butterfly. "The Maya have an inspired prophecy about the end of this cycle of time, do they not?"

"If you refer to the Tzolkín calendar, Lord," I reply, "and you

wish to discuss this matter in detail, the Chuch Kaháu is far more knowledgeable than I."

"This is one reason I am here," Kukulkán assures me gently. "I will discuss it with him. Yes. That is a time when men will again need to see the energy and hear messages of how to live. Long Reeds, you have the opportunity to participate." Kukulkán seems to be entirely absorbed in his revelations. "This is freedom of which I speak." His eyes are penetrating.

I am mesmerized by his vision. Kukulkán lies on his back. "Freedom for everyone?" I finally ask. My body collapses and I also lie back on the mat and stare up at the sky in contemplation.

Kukulkán smiles knowingly with his face toward the heavens. "First, hopefully, transformation. Then, as always, for each according to their works and according to their heart." We continue to lie on our backs, watching the towering white cloud heads drift by in silence.

fifteen

~

For the next several days, Kukulkán complies with the requests of the Halach Uinic and blesses him with prophecy for Chichén Itzá. Our site will not fall like others, but it will endure and prosper as a shining vestige of our culture, well into the new millennium. This, of course, is contingent upon several conditions: the abolition of all human sacrifice, slavery, and torture.

The Halach seems fascinated with these concepts. Chichén Itzá is already distinct from other Mayan city-states in that it is not ruled by a royal dynasty but by a triad of warrior nobleman brothers representing factions. He can foresee how these additional reforms could make Chichén a lasting star in the realm of the Yucatán.

However, his warrior brothers do not share his conviction. They each have plans of conquest, and although the Halach Uinic is the senior member of the triad rulership they hold the majority. These two sibling brothers conspire against Kukulkán's reforms, drawing on their ambitious sacrificial priesthoods, the Sharp Knives and the House of Night. The mystical Jaguar Priesthood, the Chilam Balam, and Priestesses align themselves with the Halach Uinic and Kukulkán.

One afternoon, the Halach Uinic visits the Nunnery while I am there alone. Wearing a small straw-and-feather headdress, a white waist tunic, and sandals, he enters and sits at my table. He seems quite worried about the political intrigue. "On the day of Chac in this year I am going to renounce the sacrifice due to me," he utters in a rebellious fashion, expecting me to be beholden to him. "I hope this will usher in the new era Kukulkán speaks of."

"That will be a very impressive decree," I say in awe. "You believe, then, that the moral benefits outweigh the risks?" I grab the edge of the wooden table.

"Yes, according to Kukulkán's vision."

"The price for this vision might be very high. Are you prepared to pay it?" The Halach stares back at me without replying. "This may be beneficial for you, but only if you can see it all the way through." I feel sympathy for him. "I am accustomed to paying with my life. You are not."

"I hope that I am. It has great import for the Maya. I also hope that afterward you will finally acknowledge my devotion to you," he says with genuine tenderness. I am moved to tears. "I have coveted you since the first day you were brought to me. You are the only one who soothes my soul."

I empty with rippling sadness, awestruck. His unforeseen

humility overwhelms me. I walk around the table and put my hands on his shoulders, solacing him. Although we have been perceived as arch enemies I have always understood the difference between the role and the man, and I have hoped . . .

He leaves without another word. I stand outside my door and watch heavy rain clouds move across the sky. The strong winds blow the inhabitants of Chichén like hollow reeds. A ghostlike anticipation hangs over our land. I see the Halach Uinic peering at me from every shadow, haunting me with those sad eyes, as I walk about the city talking with Kukulkán.

"I will be leaving," Kukulkán tells me the next morning as we stroll. "But that is not important. What is of lasting value has already been set in motion."

I try to put my fear aside by sitting in silence with Chon. We patiently wait until the day of the sacrifice, when the Halach Uinic will make his proclamation.

The rural Maya are flushed into the sacred city like floodwaters for the day of the offering at the holy pool of Chac. Gossiping crowds pass by the Nunnery all morning. The passage alleys between the temples, streets, and courtyards, normally open and empty, are now thronged with shuffling feet. The plan is to build future temples very high to accommodate the greater and greater influx into the city on high ceremonial days, while still providing a measure of privacy to resident ritual practitioners.

When the city is finally filled to capacity the road to the sacred pool of Chac is cleared and strewn with flowers. The Sharp Knives and the House of Night Priesthoods of the Halach brothers line the way on either side with the masses behind them. The Jaguar Priesthood circles the water.

A group of singers arrive to serenade me and escort me to the water. I am dressed in a simple white tunic with my long hair in two braids wound around my head. Chon accompanies me and we talk; people chant as we pass the observatory.

"Be prepared for anything," Chon says. We act normal, nodding our heads to the crowds we walk past. I try to look enraptured. The road is a long and narrow soft decline. When we arrive at the pool, the Halach Uinic is already there in his finest, tallest green quetzal feather headdress. He motions for us to approach the rim of the pool, and we step forward.

He takes my wrist and raises it for all to see. The crowd gasps, expecting him to begin binding my hands in preparation for throwing me into the depths. A wind kicks up.

"Here our new world begins! This offering now ends. She lives!" he shouts loudly and releases my arm. The crowd is confused. Before the Halach can explain Kukulkán's vision to the people, the two rival priesthoods push forward threateningly, filling the lane. I glance furtively at Chon, who is scanning the crowd to gauge its mood. Suddenly the mass of people part once again.

"Stand back! It's Kukulkán!" someone shouts. "Stand back!"

The people are hushed and reverent as we watch his shape slowly emerge from the crowd. I take a deep breath and grab for Chon's

hand. It is Kukulkán, his arms bound behind his back, pushed for-
ward by warriors with spears and followed by senior members of
the Sharp Knives and House of Night. Armed members of their
priesthoods now emerge from the jungle and ring the pool. They
grab the Halach Uinic. Taken by surprise, the weaponless and now
desperate members of the Jaguar Priesthood flee into the jungle. The
masses tremble in fear.

The Halach Uinic stares at me, heartbroken. Priests of the Sharp
Knives, ordered by the two lesser Halach brothers, push him to the
ground and behead the Halach Uinic on the spot with a sharp obsid-
ian sickle. They raise his blood-spurting head to the sky by its feath-
ered headdress, shouting and threatening Kukulkán. The eldest of
the rival brothers picks up the carved staff of authority from the dirt
and holds it out, claiming his dead brother's position. The crowd is
horrified and ready to scatter. I am slain with anguish and so I
scream. Kukulkán does not struggle, and the priests push him back
through the throng toward his destiny.

A huge caravan has formed to escort Kukulkán to the coast.
Soldiers of the two opposing priesthoods, with the new reigning war-
rior Halach in a litter, travel quickly through the brush that fringes
our shoreline. They push Kukulkán mercilessly through the thorny
brush, which scratches him repeatedly. Chon and I creep along at
the tail of the procession. Most of the rural Maya are flabbergasted.
They oppose this subjugation of a god and want to revolt against it,
but they are frightened and unorganized. Some begin to justify it by
saying that other gods must be partners in this overthrow. For the

time being no one seems terribly concerned about us.

When we arrive at the ocean a floating funeral pyre is quickly constructed. Kukulkán allows them to tie him to it. "I will return to you," he tells the gathered Maya, as the warriors bind him. He spies me peeping, unnoticed, from around one side of the crowd. "In the year One Reed, look for me here, where you leave me now." I struggle to push my way through the crowd to him. A guarding warrior catches me and pins my arms back. They ignite the pyre and cast Kukulkán off into the sea. I wail.

The burning pyre bobs up and down on the water, and soon my teary, unblinking eyes can no longer endure the ghastly sight. And then the pyre explodes into a blaze of light, the likes of which no one has ever seen. I am transfixed by the blaze, blown back and apart from the others by its force. The fire of transformation burns into the essence of my being, searing my forehead and then every cell of my body. The crowd watching the raging pyre is mystified and entranced. Ohhhhs round everyone's lips. They are slowed, completely stilled.

The blinding light softens into sunlight rolling through a stone window opening. I have been transported. A breeze and a gentle enveloping murmur, coming from the sparkling turquoise ocean below the white cliffs, coalesce into an ethereal awareness. I am transparent and gaze out of the window in the rippling beam of light. In the smooth sea, where I last saw Kukulkán's pyre exploding, is Chon canoeing in the spirit waters from one of the barrier islands, not far off the coast. He lands and approaches our shelter with great speed on foot, across the shifting white sands and up the soft side of the cliff.

"I saw large phantom boats," Chon tells me as he enters, shimmering.

"Where are we?" I ask.

"We are viewing past history in a place between worlds. We are traveling between bands of light."

"Are they going to land?" I ask.

"They appear to be heading north," Chon replies. "They're probably sailing for the coast closest to the Aztec capitol. They appear like a wave of ghosts."

It makes perfect sense to me. The Aztecs would now reign. They are merciless warriors. They have a calendar, yet their version ends with the third prophesied coming of Kukulkán in the year One Reed, which is now. That is almost five hundred years before the true end of the Mayan Tzolkín, which prophesies a fourth coming and the beginning of an age called the Sixth Sun of Pure Consciousness.

We begin to observe this era, watching time flow before us. Aztec merchants come and whisper to villagers that among these boat people is one who is indeed perceived by them to be godlike. He is their leader. A white-skinned bearded man, dressed in hard brilliant scales, who can separate himself at will from the tall, four-legged snorting beast with whom he is joined as one being.

Since he arrives in the year of One Reed, many Aztecs believe him to be Kukulkán or Quetzalcóatl, as they say in their Náhuatl tongue, coming in the prophesied manifestation of a war god seeking vengeance. They are confused as to how to react. Will he wreak havoc on them? Dare they risk the danger of killing another deity?

We see their emperor, Motecuzoma, sending repeated offerings of gold and precious jewels for him to leave their land. As these strangers travel inland from the coast, a flood of native people join them and march under the banner of this new god.

When the intruders reach the outskirts of Tenochtitlán, Motecuzoma has no choice but to allow them to enter and pay homage to them. But he refuses to show the leader, the one thought to be Kukulkán, his treasure storehouse.

Then something spectacular happens. The people of this entire land mass-observe two celestial omens. First there is a total solar eclipse, followed several nights later by an eerie comet that seems to hover in the darkening evening sky. It has a huge head, a long tail, and later sputters radiantly as it streaks across the blackness of the night sky. The best Zápotec, Maya, and Aztec astronomers attempt to interpret this sign.

The Aztec people intuitively realize that they are gravely mistaken about the intent of the newcomers. It is now certain that whoever this being may be, his coming will be fatal to their universe. They hide their treasure and therefore finally engage in a bloody battle, fought to the death by almost every Aztec man, woman, and child in the city.

The Español—as he calls himself—a supposed god and conqueror of the Aztec race, this total antithesis of Kukulkán, is Hernando

Cortés: a demon who arrives in the year One Reed and who sends his lackey, Pedro de Alvarado, south to conquer the Maya.

When the second wave of invaders arrive with their beasts Chon and I cross the energetic barrier and are more present in this reality, which appears to be some kind of hell. We are in awe of them. They use armor that is heavy and noisy and their bodies stink underneath it. The smell of their breath is putrid from eating sour meat. They are thin, pale, and have hairy faces. The animals, however, are fine, glossy and beautiful, large and arrogant, strong and high-spirited.

They enter the town of Tulum with their ragged band, abusing the population and demanding to know where to find more of the yellow metal. They yell in broken Aztec. The whole village is occupied. The local ruler is held captive in his chambers. He tells them in his Mayan-accented Aztec that the village has no yellow metal. All that they possessed was traded long ago. The oppressors make slaves of the men. Maya are forced to haul their heavy chests to spare their beasts. People are questioned about the location of ancient cities and tortured when no one reveals anything. These horrors continue until the invaders are partially satisfied and go off in search of more booty. They promise to return to establish their own government, to which all will have to submit.

When the next band of Españoles arrive they look different from these warriors. I am almost fooled, but underneath they are the same devils. They dress in brown hooded robes and carry the crossed sticks that Kukulkán foresaw. The Padres, as they call themselves, have been scouring the Mayan lands to confiscate and burn sacred books. When Chon hears of this atrocity, he hides more than two hundred volumes under a trap door in the small shelter we are occupying.

The villagers, minus the many men taken captive, walk out to greet the new intruders with a jaundiced eye. As a gesture of goodwill the Padres pass out woven blankets to all the villagers. They tell them that they are going to establish a community and that they want the villagers to accept their god Jesu Cristo.

The Padres next build a wooden structure topped with their crossed sticks. They observe the agricultural methods and talk to the people about the book of their god. During their stay, we hear many rumors from other parts of the land about these people and the disease that follows in their wake. Then some of the Maya in the village break out with small festering sores.

At first only a few people become ill, but it quickly spreads to nearly the whole population of Tulum. The sickness does not subside with time but rather the body becomes increasingly covered with nasty, oozing boils. They are very painful and are accompanied by a high fever. No one knows what to make of it.

When the first person dies Chon brings out his medicinal vapors and herbs to see if he can heal them, but he cannot stop the spread of the vile disease. We keep experimenting with new remedies, while people die all around us.

I walk into a dark hut where an old man is agonizing. Throughout the hanging, undulating shadows I can hear him whimpering, and there is a sickly, still smell in the airless energy, like sulfur fumes. Outside there is no one working the fields, and the Padres spend all their time in the wooden dwelling, reading the book of Jesu Cristo.

"Is he going to die, Chon?" I ask in a soft whisper. The man is giving up the ghost. Chon fans him with copal smoke. He then pours sips of a hot yellow herbal brew into the man's gaping, moaning mouth.

Chon squats on his haunches and turns to me with a tired, worried look on his face. "This is more than just death. It is beyond witchery or petty evil. I have never seen anything like it before. It is a second death. Heaven knows what these people are going through when they leave this realm, if they ever do." He puts his head in his hands.

People are entering death all around us. The living are fearful about disposing of the massive numbers of corpses. Huge bonfires are built, but the villagers tremble at the thought that the disease might even be carried on the smoke. The Padres believe that the illness was brought with the blankets and order all of them to be burned, but it is too late. This is the wrath of unrequited life force.

Chon works tirelessly but without success. The Padres jabber on to the dying about accepting Jesu Cristo before death. Some of the villagers agree in desperation. They are anointed with oil and allow a small white wafer to be placed in their mouths, but there is no relief.

When nearly everyone has died and the Padres are considering leaving, I feel a pox on my forehead. I look, panic-stricken, at Chon. He has one on his face and several on his arms as well. I am horrified.

"Chon! How can this be happening? The illness has broken through the barrier! Are we also going to die?" I gasp. "I don't want to die this way!"

"That is not all, either," he says. "The conquerors have decimated the people. There may not be enough knowledge left to ensure our culture's continuation. We have to save whatever we can, Merilyn." Chon's face fractures with sadness.

We hear the sound of the Padres approaching. They burst into our shelter and begin to accuse Chon of bringing this plague on by hoarding the books of the Diablo. The Padres are furious and ransack the room, moving a straw mat covering the trap door.

An evil smile crosses their faces. They greedily retrieve the two-hundred-plus volumes from the underground hiding place. Thumbing through them, they laugh at the hieroglyphs and numbers and toss the books like trash into a big pile in front of the doorway.

Chon and I stare at each other with dread, while they prepare to burn the books. "Without our knowledge, we might not return!" he tells me. I recoil as the Padres light kindling around centuries of treasured wisdom.

"Memory comes from within," Chon finally says, peering transfixed at the growing blaze. "Do you trust me?"

I nod my head yes. He grabs my hand. We make a fierce dash out of the door and jump into the bonfire.

The center has not ignited yet, but there is flesh-crisping heat ringed by roaring flames. My nostrils and lungs burn with smoke. We stand there, huddled against one another, on top of our mound of burning knowledge and history. The Padres scream at us and pray for salvation. What we have done is so wholly "other" to them.

As I hear them cry in horror there is an explosion of light within the ring of fire and I am standing on the burning funeral pyre before Kukulkán. It is he and I who now blaze, surrounded by flames. Chon is gone. Kukulkán picks up a book from the ignited pile that rages around us. He holds the book out to me until I take it from his hand. Then he smiles, and we explode into another blinding flash.

I awakened in the cold stream above the ruins of Palenque. I was lying on my back, completely immersed in water. Dawn was breaking and both Chon and don Juan were at my side, trying to revive me. I stared up into the weatherworn face and thick white hair of don Juan, who was smiling down at me.

"We'd better get out of here," Chon said. "It will be morning soon and this scene would create a stir. Can you walk, Merilyn?"

"I can't even move," I managed to mumble. Don Juan and Chon each took one of my drenched arms. They lifted me up rather easily, which surprised me but should not have.

When they saw that I was unable to walk, don Juan, with the strength of a lumberjack, hoisted me onto his back and we began to walk away. He carried me piggyback for almost a mile up a mild incline.

I was overwhelmed by the power and determination of this ninety-eight-year-old Indian man. I wrapped my arms around his neck and shoulders and buried my face in his white hair. I sensed myself basking in the force of his presence.

"Don't leave me, don Juan," I said to him. I felt don Juan's warrior's intent could have carried me up the steepest mountains of Tibet, gleaming as white as the shimmering hair on his eaglelike head.

I was Heidi riding on the back of my grandfather as the sun rose over the jungle. The morning's floral rainbows awoke to trumpet and unfold erotically. This was surreal life and awareness, ever changing. The thick rain forest fragrances tried to draw me to their lush centers as my head spun, and I spiraled into them. A giant lime-green butterfly fluttered the dance of light, and my cheek lolled on my arm as I followed it.

When we arrived back at Esmeralda's place, Chon deposited me in the curing hut. I immediately fell asleep. My dreams were very sad and fragile, like dewy drops of captured birdsong suspended in a spider's web, or vibrating harp strings in the moaning breeze.

sixteen

◠

Chon and don Juan realized that I needed time alone. My glassy eyes poured rivers of tears as I watched Kukulkán's world pass away through the mist, dissolving. I released the last fleeting images of the Halach Uinic and the bonfire that destroyed the Mayan sacred books. Quite frankly, I just wanted to die. I curled up in a fetal position for days in my hammock, while Chon and don Juan brought me food, hoping I would eat.

Little Manik jumped around, concerned, trying to bring me back to life but with little success. Don Juan played his flute at night, and I did respond to its haunting, longing melodies. I wondered, as I listened to the flute, what was in the book that Kukulkán handed me. What could it possibly contain? And I knew that its secret was imbued in me.

After watching my condition worsen, Chon and don Juan decided that we needed to talk about my overpowering emotions to prevent them from completely shutting me down. I did not know where to begin, but their insistence finally broke through to me.

"How is this all possible?" I finally asked.

"It's the times," Chon said. "It's possible. We all have moments when we become more than is conceivable. It raises us up."

"Am I going to die now?" I breathed in deeply and lifted my hand to my mouth.

"It's when we feel life can slip away that we often stand up and start to live. That's what's happening now," insisted don Juan.

"What about the Halach Uinic?" I was overflowing with feelings.

Chon closed his eyes. "When he was asked to pay the price, he couldn't."

"But he died!"

He opened his eyes. "Resenting it with his dying breath." Chon soothed me. "In his own way he cared for you, which is part of what you're feeling now. He knew it was better to end it for himself. Maybe he learned something."

I gulped, sensing that Chon was right.

"It's to your credit that you even care," don Juan said with disdain. "If this is what it takes for someone to learn, I say piss on 'em." We all had a good laugh for the first time since our return. Chon snickered, his hand in front of his mouth.

"What did you see that night, Chon?" I asked him, although I was afraid his answer might make me even more depressed.

"I saw how this current culture uses technology as a crutch for its energy, but not in the same way a lame person might use a wheelchair to move about more easily. The wheelchair is a concentrating, limitation-defying challenge. Technology is an opiate, since it has not yet freed the energy of the many for other pursuits. This present culture is feeble, but perhaps that is good, for look at the havoc it has wrought. It remembers little of what other cultures were, and knows less of what we might yet be.

"I saw this illness you have as a great opening. One does not need defenses. One needs to release into the flow and allow energy to imbue. The Earth and energy itself do not have to support what we are if we fight them off. Humans, for all their value, have to learn how to live in balance with everything else. For all their urges, they must see that just wanting and having is not enough. Beyond that, of course, they have to care for one another.

"I then glimpsed formulas for future evolution and realized that perhaps you should write down your experiences and speak out."

"What good could it possibly do?" I fretted. Manik made a mopey face.

Chon smirked. "Write it and see what happens. Maybe something. You're a fine woman, highborn and educated. People will not expect this voice to come from you, someone who should be thrilled and contented with all the honors you have acquired." Chon gazed at his hand as if admiring a ring. "Someone who should have been sheltered from all of this. People will not anticipate your feelings for other cultures or your grasp of other realities and may contemplate how such a thing can be. They will wonder at your stories and your illness, your kind of Dreaming, and your lack of anger. Perhaps others will remember. Perhaps some people will see. Or it is possible that all will just dry up and blow away like a dust devil in the wind, leaving behind only emptiness without the presence of spirit to guide life. But either way you will be free."

"I can't expect it to change anything," I responded, looking deeply into don Juan's brown eyes.

"Maybe that's as it should be."

"What did you see, don Juan?"

"I saw how awareness is retreating from form," he said, pinching his arm's flesh to indicate matter, "because of the way we are abusing both. It does not have to be that way, but that is the way things are moving. I also saw the kind of energy, mind, and heart it takes to exist well in a world without form. Most people don't have the mettle, and that is why they fear the coming change. Yet in the meantime, they devalue and destroy the only physical world we currently have and repress the spirit, all because of this lack in them. This world's value is our bridge into other realms and our very existence. I then saw where we might go when we leave here. I saw us explode together into the infinite," he finished.

I was breathless at the beauty and totality of their visions.

"What did you see?" they both asked with wonder, again in unison, exchanging looks and laughing.

I recounted my entire experience from beginning to end. They were completely engrossed and seemed particularly interested in the chamber of the light beings.

"So you communicated with them?" Chon asked in fascination.

"Yes."

In turn they each revealed that during their visions they had also entered into the golden dome of the light beings. Chon explained that it was an evolutionary experience evoked by the sacred mushrooms.

"I have heard the hippies that used to come around here say that the ancient Maya raised their vibrations and departed into other dimensions or even into other universes or UFOs," Chon giggled. "It's not silly, but it sounds that way, the way they say it. Now you can both see they were right."

We all burst into hysterical laughter. It felt good to laugh so hard and experience the release. Manik tried to steal the moment of good spirits by claiming the attention for himself. He jumped up and down holding his sexual organ. That sent us rolling on the floor.

"This is what we are working with." Don Juan aped Manik, jutting his jaw at the monkey, on whom the joke, but not the excitement, was lost.

"Tell us, Merilyn," Chon asked, when the hilarity had settled down to titters, "what is the thing you remember most about Kukulkán?"

"Everything, really." I paused for a moment. "The freedom. The vision. A giving nature of love. Transcendence. The . . . explosion." I held back my tears. "He gave me a book. I wasn't sure if I should take it. Now I just wish I could read what it said." We were all silent for a while. "It was one of our own books but somehow transformed."

"Maybe you will decode it," don Juan replied cryptically. "And as for your illness, I know this sounds eerie and daring but I don't think you should worry about it. Something is going on here. It ought to speak for itself. Let's listen to it."

Chon nodded his head in respectful acknowledgement, as did I, looking deeply again into don Juan's fierce but kind eyes. Chon and don Juan each gave me deep hugs, and I spent the rest of the day feeling quiet, stilled, and hopeful.

We passed the remaining days of my visit in a state of grace. Chon took us to the Misol Ha falls, a high mountain river of virgin water that cascades the purest aquamarine. We also visited Nahá, the last settlement of true jungle Maya, who still speak the original dialect of Palenque as it was spoken at its height some thirteen hundred years ago. The jungle was being cleared around them, and there were only two hundred or so of the people left but they remained, still wearing their white tunics. The old wise man Chan Kin Viejo said he was glad to see us.

From Nahá we paddled in a dugout canoe down the Usumacinta River into Guatemala and viewed the ruins of Chon's home, Tikal. I was not familiar with this site, but for Chon it was a glorious experience, moving beyond words. The greatest spectacle was the main pyramid, the gem of Tikal, the highest structure I had ever seen in the world of the Maya.

We journeyed into the surrounding mountain regions, where the Maya had fled the Spaniards in the 1600s. The towns here had a decidedly colonial feel, but the houses were still all Yotoch. Women sat at back-strap looms, weaving designs that had been worn for more than two thousand years.

Traveling back toward Palenque we boarded our old familiar train and headed into the Yucatán toward Chichén Itzá. When we went as far as we could by rail the three of us got off and took a bus the rest of the way.

The site was still as immense as I remembered it. The

massive pyramid to Kukulkán had been partially restored by the Mexican government. However, all the terra cotta coloring had worn away and had not yet been replaced. I doubted that it would ever be restored. Today they would not know how to color the reliefs.

We walked down to the sacred well and sat there a long time while the wind picked up and blew around us. The water was greener than I remembered. Just above the well a small thatch stand sold fresh pineapple juice, attended by young Mayan women dressed colorfully in embroidered blouses. They greeted people mostly in their own dialect, with a few words of accented Spanish or English for the tourists.

After spending a few hours there we strolled back to the main section of the former city. Along with Chon and don Juan, I climbed to the top of the Temple to the Warriors. The giant Chac Mool still reclined there with his huge belly plate empty. At the back of the upper temple was the stone slab where offerings were made, and the chamber from which the Halach Uinic would emerge. I ran my hand across the stone.

At the bottom we rambled among the thousand crumbling columns that circled the temple, and then made our way down the path toward the observatory. Its roof had been partially eroded, exposing the coiled interior. It looked like an ancient snail shell washed up by the primordial sea.

Across from it were the ruins of the Nunnery. Chon and I walked inside, and he pretended to light a wall torch while

I sat down on the floor. The stone arches seemed low to me and the rock appeared ancient, yet (if I closed my eyes) I could still visualize the furnishings in the sleep chamber around the corner.

In a rented Volkswagen I drove us down the coast toward Tulum. There was no sign of the wooden church built by the missionaries. A pair of large iguanas were sunning themselves on boulders at the cliffs. Below were miles of unspoiled beach, rolling like waves in the light of the sun. The jungle palms were swaying in the breeze. We found the sparkling Caribbean irresistible, and we tumbled down the sandy slope, stripping to our undergarments and plunging in for a swim.

Climbing back up the slope, I found a conch shell trumpet and a small clay butterfly imbedded in the sand. That evening we went to a local fish place for a sea fare feast; the three of us were absolutely giddy. We clowned, laughed, and pounded on the table for more food. The waitresses, local Mayan girls, appeared delighted by our antics, gossiping cheerfully about us behind the counter.

The next morning we boarded a multicolored Mexican second-class bus, complete with a Virgin Mary and fuzzy dice dangling from the rearview mirror. We rode back up the coast to Xcaret, the site of the sacred ritual baths. The dolphins still swam in the crystal-clear water, as did a large variety of beautiful tropical fish. We waded in and floated in the underground caverns, illuminated by sunbeam spot-lights that dove in from round celestial holes above.

That evening we arrived in Uxmal, the ancient Maya's university city. We watched the swallows fly around the ruins until twilight and watched the courtyard and pyramid shine with the colors of a beautiful Mexican sunset. As we walked among the structures, Chon reminded me that the teachers had to be fifty years old before they could reside in Uxmal permanently, and that these grand instructors wore giant sea turtle shells as ornamental breastplates to symbolize the wisdom of longevity.

That night we dreamed, we flew, and we remembered. The next day we started the bus trip back to Palenque. Although still sleepy, I remained awake in my seat so as not to miss one of these last moments with them. Don Juan pointed out several soaring hawks through the window as we rode along.

When we arrived the following afternoon at Palenque, Esmeralda had just returned and there was a party atmosphere at the restaurant until closing. Esmeralda patted me joyously between the shoulders every time we passed, and the three of us sat in the kitchen and talked with her while she cooked.

We recounted our trip to the different Mayan sites, while we all gorged ourselves on Esmeralda's sumptuous meal. Afterwards we talked late into the night, sitting around a fire to keep the mosquitoes away. As we were breaking up don

Juan said that he would charter a flight back to Mexico City for the day after tomorrow. That brought me back to reality, making me a little sad as I excused myself and went to bed.

I Dream of a beautiful river of light, flowing musically throughout the heavens like the Milky Way. I rise up to it and step across as my feet dissolve. On the other side is an illuminated land, rather like a higher plane of Earth. I walk a long time alone before I see the shapes of individuals who may not leave the banks. There, they must sit and gaze woefully into the mirrorlike waters, watching all the passing wasted images for an eternity or until they spiral downward.

Some free beings come out to meet me and escort me to another place. Their bodies are light and golden and at peace. They have high, oblong heads. We come to a sacred pool, a spiraling, shimmering vortex. This is the place where one is called forth, and it is ringed with angels: beautiful moving lights, ethereal sound vibrations, and ministering emotions. The angels call like howling wolves into the vortex. Their sound reaches its outer limits, and they show me how to sing at the pool.

They tell me that as a woman I can pull lost life from the vortex and demonstrate how to reach into its spinning core. It is simply my own creative energy and my longing in combination with the vortex that cause the desired beloveds to emerge out of it. I am entranced, and they tell me that I may stay there as long as I desire. I feel that if I were to stay for an eternity I would become the keeper of this sacred pool.

I call forth the image of Richard and then of my great-grand-mother, of don Juan and Chon, then of the Halach Uinic and finally of lost Coyol. I see them free, beautiful, perfect, and surrounded by healing and blessing energies. "I love you," I say.

Then the angels tell me to jump in myself. When I do I completely dissolve in the pool's energy. They call out and emit rays of light into the waters. That heats the waters, causing them to bubble and shoot up like a geyser. I am in the midst of this whirling ascension tube of liquid light.

When I step out I can connect with many people, those who have helped me, those I have wanted to help. Spirits come to me with messages. I thank the angels and then lower myself back through the watery tunnel of light to my body on Earth and reenter through the crown and the heart.

In the morning Chon was waiting for me at the breakfast table, wanting to spend time together. We ate quietly while don Juan relaxed in a hammock hung under the mangoes. Esmeralda did not open the restaurant this day. Later we all went to town for an afternoon movie at the only cinema. It was a rather unusual Chinese film, featuring a family of circus acrobats.

That night we dined at a restaurant in town, making quite a festive spectacle of ourselves. Esmeralda wore a colorful new dress, and I the best skirt and blouse I had brought with me. Afterwards we took a lively walk to the square under the waning moon. We sat on benches and laughed, watching the balloon vendors, listening to the folk harp players, and eating peddled treats like roasted corn ears and slices of fresh coconut.

It was late when we returned to Esmeralda's place, and after the men went to sleep I asked her if she would cut my hair. She went for a basin of water and a pair of scissors, while I sat in a straight-backed chair under a tall avocado tree.

"Are you sure you want to do this?" she asked. "Your long hair is so pretty."

"I'm sure," I said. "It's difficult for me to maintain now. Braid it in two." I looked down at the basin of water in which the last quarter of the moon was reflected.

She nodded her head. "How short do you want it?" she asked, combing my long strands with a wet comb.

"To about the collarbone," I replied. "And give me bangs. Egyptian-style." I laughed.

"Also like some Maya," she giggled and began to whack away at the front.

"Esmeralda, why do you think Chon never married?" I asked her with the curiosity of a child.

She looked into my eyes tolerantly, while the night lights were reflected in hers. "Oh, well, many healers never marry. It's too much work, and it takes tremendous energy. But if you want to know about his women, I think he likes them young." We both laughed. She braided one side, cut it off, undid it and trimmed it up. Then she stood back to admire the difference. "Not bad," she said. "And he likes the ones like you the best," she added, as she went to work on the other side. I blushed badly.

We created two bundles out of my cut braids, tying them up in colored pieces of satin that she had stashed away to make embroidered pouches. She now brought out a looking glass and hung it on the tree next to the rain barrel so that I could appreciate her handiwork. I had to admit that it was an improvement in that it made me look younger. I contemplated cutting it shorter still.

At breakfast the next morning, after the surprised but pleasant comments about my hair, Esmeralda pretended to take pictures of us with an empty camera. We stood posing pompously in different groupings between moments of hysterical laughter. The rest of the morning passed slowly while I packed. Chon came into the hut while I was stuffing my duds into a suitcase. "I don't know if I can bear this," I whispered to him.

He sat down in a hammock. "It's very difficult. I find myself wishing it didn't have to be this way. Why couldn't it be somebody else for this task? But if it weren't you, we wouldn't be together in this manner."

"I don't want to leave!"

"You must go back until you get this thing done. Do you know what to do?" he asked, rubbing his forehead.

"Yes," I said. "I really do."

"That's good." He smiled. "When it's completed, remember: You belong with us." I ran over and embraced him for what seemed like an eternity. Then I gave him the package with one of my cut braids and did not feel silly about it.

"Do you want to take Manik?" he asked, hastily wiping his eye. "He would like to help you."

"I don't think I could get him into the country."

"Same with me," Chon reflected. "Still, take his intent. Do you know this Mayan phrase?"

I recalled the meaning of his words whispered softly in Maya. "Overcomes Death?"

"Same with you," Chon smiled. We closed my suitcase and smiled at each other.

It was about 3:00 P.M. and time for us to leave. Chon turned his back to us as we stepped off the property and piled into a rented jeep. Then he about-faced and waved as we drove away. Don Juan and I were very quiet. The wind blew through our hair. We were both trying not to look back.

The charter flight was exceptionally beautiful. Aloft we asked the pilot to circle the ruins and since he was part Maya he obliged us. The view of the temples from the air was like something from another world, as if they had been laid out by the gods themselves according to a master plan. Their grandeur, solemnity, steadfastness, and seclusion was absolutely mystical. I said good-bye to them for the time being.

Esmeralda had supplied don Juan with a bag of tamales, which we shared on the flight to Mexico City. There were yucca tamales with almonds, pineapple with raisins, and wild turkey with pumpkin seed sauce. I laid my head on don Juan's shoulder as we cruised through the clouds.

Soon we landed amid the terrific bustle of the Mexico City airport. I held onto don Juan's hand for dear life, for fear that someone in the crowd might separate us and take him away from me. It did not happen. While waiting for my flight we sat down and talked in a coffee shop.

"I know how you feel," don Juan said over a glass of mineral water. "We felt like this in the beginning times on the reservations. We still do. It is like you're being ripped away from everything you love, everything that stands for you."

I nodded my head.

"What is there for you where you're going?" he asked, tipping his bottle to see if there was any water left and then ordering another bottle from the waiter.

"Nothing but memories and duties. Those people don't understand me well. It is empty."

"An ideal situation. Your friends will come through for you, though," don Juan said. "I'm sure of it. Your fiancé was from that place, wasn't he?"

"You remember Richard?" I asked him, stunned that he recalled this old story from so long ago.

"Of course," he answered. "He helped bring you to me,

remember? Now he will guide you again and help you survive being home awhile."

"It is just like me having to depend on a dead fiancé for support," I said.

Don Juan smirked. "Don't underestimate any help from the spirit world, Merilyn."

"Spoken like a true Indian."

"At your service," he smiled, and we both had a laugh. I gave him the other bundle with my braid in it.

"I'll remember you," he said, taking the hair and putting it in the breast pocket of his blue shirt.

I paid for my ticket. Curiously, don Juan did not purchase one. We sat in the terminal and waited for my flight to be called. After an hour, don Juan walked me to the gateway, complete with a metal detector. He could go no further.

I experienced tremendous anxiety about walking through the gate and leaving without don Juan. I held on to him until I imagined everybody in the airport had stopped to gawk at us. We actually glowed with a yellowish oval of light as we embraced, and there was a timeless silence, a hum. When we pulled away from the hug, I saw that no one had even noticed us.

"You see? Just a wooden Indian to them," he said.

I smiled at him. As I cautiously walked through the gate, I sensed a flash of light behind me. I frantically turned around, but don Juan had disappeared from where he was standing only a moment ago.

The plane was late taking off, which was not that uncommon for the Mexico City airport. I sat in my seat wondering about Chon and don Juan. Finally, the emotional drain of the parting took its toll, and I drifted off into a light, flying sleep.

I Dream of the three of us together in Nahá, canoeing down the sparkling Usumacinta River toward a spot in the water that is strewn with flowers. There, waiting for us in another canoe, floating upon the petals, is Kukulkán. He is smiling.

I Dream that I am again in the highlands of Chiapas and the dancing priest is walking into the mist wearing the white stone mask given to me by the sacred jaguar. I catch up with him and tap him on the left shoulder. He turns around and I take my mask from his face, dropping his to the ground on the snow. Behind the sacred white stone mask is a glowing light void. I bow and back away through the misty vortex of Dreaming.

Perhaps Chon is right, that in writing I will decode what is written in the sacred book Kukulkán gave me. That would be wonderful!

Epilogue

~

As to our progress in decoding the *Book of Kukulkán*, as of the revision of this book, we now understand that it deals with evolutionary transformation and on this we have been tirelessly focused. We have now been able to open the book in Dreaming and have found four known characters within it. In the waking world of science, the *Book of Life* has, in fact, also been opened, as of June 23, 2000, and has been found to contain four genetic characters, represented in one billion five hundred million pieces of genetic code, intricately and reciprocally combined.

We have also discovered something that the scientists have not, that there is a fifth character, a heretofore unknown letter of the existential alphabet, the addition of which causes the entirety of creation to "read out" differently. It changes the meaning of every single line or nonlinear combination. This is not a mutation, which is formed by inserting an extra representative or a representative strand of any of the four known characters, but rather is something completely different that appears to lead into a mysterious evolutionary opportunity.

As a result of this discovery, we have also recently learned that there are four categories of illness. The first category will heal itself naturally, so nonharmful medical or energetic intervention is redundant. The second category can be cured if the proper medicine can be found. It often requires both appropriate medical and suitable energetic intervention. The third category cannot be cured. This is due to the energetic debts of the being or the lineage. It will be fatal, but if these debts are paid the life may be extended and its quality may be improved. The fourth type of illness is of a purely energetic nature and will respond only to the appropriate energetic measures.

We are in the process of understanding which illnesses pertain to which categories. We have, for example, learned an amazing fact: that HIV pertains to the second rather than to the third category of illness. Additionally we have seen that cancer may pertain to category two or to category three and that this is dependent on the specific energetic scenario.

We have discovered that there are methods for discerning the category to which an illness belongs, so that the appropriate measures—medical and/or energetic—may be taken or sought out. This discernment is a necessary tool in dealing with unwellness and in having total certainty as to the course of action.

We have also explored how this new element, combined with skilled Dreaming and the appropriate intent, beneficially affects accurate diagnosis, the search for and the application of cures and treatments, the ability to survive, and the quality of life. Overall, we feel that this may be a completely new dimension in the universe of well-being, evolution, and transformation.

We are able to "see" outcomes accurately and with complete clarity, even given the complex energetic situations and the intricate challenges that life faces in these times. This has afforded us the capacity to serve as good counsel. There is reason for hope and yet there is much need for dedication, hard work, and sobriety.

It is my sincere wish that humanity wake up to these and other wondrous possibilities, to those that facilitate realization and an end to suffering. Anything is possible, yet we must understand why we would want or need something to be and then, based upon such understanding, accurately discern if this is selfless, necessary, loving, transcendental, and ultimately liberating.

Afterthoughts

~

Many people who meet me, who read my books or attend my workshops or speaking events ask me one simple question. "How did you do it?" They are referring to my emotional healing, in the hopes that I can help them find their own path, which sometimes I am able to do.

Basically, I have only one brief answer, which can be summed up in four letters. Love. The simple truth is that I love with an irrepressible audacity, sincerely, with joy and abandon.

I wish that I could be more specific, but a definiton of true love is hard to come by. Don Juan once said, "To the riddle of life, there is but one answer. In the end, one must love enough to give back in a pure form everything that one has been given, and more besides in the form of gratitude, and still have more than one started with."

I will quote one wiser and greater than I in this matter. My heart has always honestly sought love as the proper way to live, and I have loved, as such, fearlessly and spontaneously, at times more than I ever thought possible. I can say that genuine love has never failed to demonstrate itself to be the most generous, most benevolent way of being, even in a world filled with death.

Genuine love, however, cannot be faked, not from within. One must be willing to put the "self" or the ego on the line. There is an altruism and a harmlessness to genuine love that is absolutely sublime. Yet true love is fiercely loyal and radically faithful, though inwardly compassionate, forgiving, and very kind. Such a gentle yet powerful inner state is simply not conducive to anything that will ultimately defeat one's journey, and so one flies into the infinite on the wings of hope, peerless passion and pure intent.

This is a great art and a great secret. I hope you can or come to understand it.

About the Author

~

Merilyn Tunneshende, M.Ed., has studied the energetic practices of shamans for twenty-three years and holds degrees in Language, Comparative Religion/Philosophy, and Education. She is the author of two books on Dreaming and other shamanic practices.

Ms. Tunneshende has spoken at symposiums and conferences with noted psychiatrists, scientists, and physicians on topics ranging from love to shamanism, alternative medicine, and traditional Western medicine. She conducts experimental events in which she shares some of the practices and insights from her books and ongoing work.

Books of Related Interest

The Teachings of Don Carlos
Practical Applications of the Works of Carlos Castaneda
by Victor Sanchez

The Toltec Path of Recapitulation
Healing Your Past to Free Your Soul
by Victor Sanchez

Mastery of Awareness
Living the Agreements
by Doña Bernadette Vigil with Arlene Broska, Ph.D.

Spirit of the Shuar
Wisdom from the Last Unconquered People of the Amazon
by John Perkins and Shakaim Mariano Shakai Ijisam Chumpi

Dance of the Four Winds
Secrets of the Inca Medicine Wheel
by Alberto Villoldo and Erik Jendresen

Island of the Sun
Mastering the Inca Medicine Wheel
by Alberto Villoldo and Erik Jendresen

The Sexual Teachings of the White Tigress
Secrets of the Female Taoist Masters
by Hsi Lai

The Illustrated Kama Sutra
Ananga-Ranga • Perfumed Garden
Translated by Sir Richard Burton and F. F. Arbuthnot

Inner Traditions • Bear & Company
P.O. Box 388 • Rochester, VT 05767
1-800-246-8648 • www.InnerTraditions.com
Or contact your local bookseller